CHROMATOGRAPHY

An Adventure

GUY ALEXANDER

AMERICAN CHEMICAL SOCIETY

Washington, D.C. 1977

Library of Congress CIP Data

Alexander, Guy B.

Chromatography.
(Chemistry in action)

Includes bibliographic references and index.

1. Alexander, Guy B. 2. Chemists—Biography. 3.
Wisconsin. University—Graduate work. 4. Chromato-
graphic analysis.
I. Title.

QD22.A385A34   543'.08   77-8637
ISBN 0-8412-0277-X   1–165   (1977)

To Mary, with love

This book is dedicated to Mary, my wife, who shared
the excitement of graduate school with me, who never
doubted even when life looked impossible, and who
always had a smile and a friendly word for all who
crossed our path.

Acknowledgment

To the Rohm and Haas Company for samples of Amberite IR–4B and their literature on ion exchange, I express my thanks. The Glossary of Ion Exchange is theirs, and many of the figures are also theirs.

I also wish to express my appreciation to Professor V. W. Meloche. He taught me many things about life and work and honesty, and he did much to make my stay at Wisconsin happy, friendly, and profitable. He forced me to think independently and work independently. He taught me by pointing to the road and then letting me take the journey even if I made mistakes.

Prior to my study with ion exchange resins, neither the Professor nor I had any experience with chromatography. I shall be ever grateful that the Professor allowed me to work out the details by myself. So many professors are not like that. One of the professors I knew had his graduate students for Thanksgiving dinner and immediately following the meal he led them back to the laboratory. Professor Meloche was not like that. When Mary and I and the other graduate students went to his home for a holiday, we left feeling that he and Mrs. Meloche had been wonderful hosts and that we had had a real holiday with our friends.

In one respect my adventure in graduate research was really not typical because it was my adventure, done for my development, and not under the drive of a publication hungry professor who used his students like galley slaves. So, to Professor Meloche, many thanks for letting me grow and develop in my own way.

I thank Dr. Conard Fernelius for helping me over some of the rough spots in the manuscript. And thanks to Robert F. Gould of the American Chemical Society for his demonstration of paper chromatography, which, after minor revision, is now a part of the story of chapter two.

Most of all, I wish to thank Mary for sharing the experience with me.

CONTENTS

Preface

This book is written for young students who wonder what a career in science is really like. It is also written for those who think they would like to go to graduate school and are wondering what kinds of things life as a graduate student brings. Finally, it is written for those who have heard about chromatography and wonder just what chromatography is.

As a teenager I was excited by the discovery of nylon, and I wanted to be a chemist and invent things. I was awed by the older fellows from our small town who went away to college and completely overwhelmed by one who went on to graduate school. I figured that he was the smartest young man in the whole world; I put him in a class with Einstein.

I wondered what it would be like to sit in a class room in graduate school and hear lectures from the smartest scientists in the world. When the chance came for me to go to Wisconsin, I was like a young boy at Christmas. When the opportunity came to write a book on chromatography, the subject of my thesis, I decided to do two things simultaneously: describe chromatography and describe my experiences in graduate school in the form of an autobiography.

Had I done this in 1947 when I graduated, there would have been no problem, but now, 29 years later, there is one: namely, the growth of science in the past two and a half decades. For example, how could one write a book on chromatography today and leave out gas chromatography? Another author might have solved the problem easily, but for me there seemed to be no solution until I hit on the idea of writing a part of the book as though it had just happened.

So here it is, the story of my graduate school experiences partially fictionized, to bring the science of chromatography more nearly up to date. Chapters two, eight, nine, and eleven, particularly, have been modernized. It is still the kind of thing that did happen to me and the kind of story that could be happening in graduate school today, the kind of thing that could happen to you if you decide to go to graduate school.

One more thing, the characters of the book are based on real people, real as seen through my eyes, many years ago, but partly fictitious.

CHAPTER 1

Wisconsin

Sleep was impossible. I looked at the clock. 6:00 a.m. Mary was sleeping soundly beside me. I rolled over trying to find a comfortable spot, yet being careful not to wake her up. When I couldn't stand it any longer, I got up and looked out the window. So this is Madison, Wisconsin, I thought. And out there somewhere is the University.

I felt confident and scared all at once. My hands were clammy and my face felt sweaty. Out there was the university. How would it treat me? Demandingly? Friendly? Impossibly? Would I, as some of my peers had done, go home in a few months, defeated, beaten, whipped by the rigors of graduate school? Or would I graduate, and be called Dr. Alexander for the rest of my life?

I dressed, drank a glass of milk, and then started for the campus, for the chemistry building, for my new life. I got there at 7:30. Professor Meloche, the man who was to be my major professor, hadn't arrived, so I waited in the hall outside his office. I didn't have a watch; I'm not really sure how long I waited, but it seemed hours. I guess the reason it seemed so long was partly the suspense connected with a new situation, partly because I was anxious to get started, and partly because I was curious to learn what kind of thesis problem he'd assigned to me. Mentally, I added the title to my name, Guy B. Alexander, Ph.D. I wondered if it would ever be, or if, like so many others, I'd be a casualty.

1

A number of the stories I had heard about graduate schools passed through my mind. One of my colleagues at Utah, a fellow who had always been a standout in his class, had gone to a graduate school in the Midwest and lasted only six months. Claude said he hadn't failed; he said he just couldn't take the slavery, working every night past midnight and weekends too. To make matters worse, Claude said, his professor had held back his pay. Not only that, but Claude also reported that there was a graduate student who'd been around for five years and still didn't have any idea when he'd finish. My friend couldn't see spending five years to get a Ph.D. It was a fantastic story, and I wondered if it wasn't a case of sour grapes because he had gotten a professor he didn't like, or if he had really just flunked out.

I had heard all kinds of stories about the qualifying examinations—about how hard they were and how many flunked because of them, and then the language exams and, of course, the defense of the thesis.

I was so involved with my thoughts that I didn't know when the professor came.

It seemed to me that he was unusually gruff. He told me where to register and that I should come back to his office as soon as I was finished. He reminded me that school would start in a couple of days, and that there wasn't much time to get settled.

It took me over two hours to register. I don't know how many times I got lost, and the worst part of it was that every time I asked for directions, I was treated like a freshman. I remember paying the fees and counting my money. All I had left was two dollars and ten cents. And pay wouldn't come for over a month.

It was almost lunch time when I returned to Professor Meloche's office. It was locked. I wandered down the hall. The supply room was open, so I stopped to ask the fellow there if anyone had seen the professor.

"I'm Ralph Helmke," he said, evading my question. "You must be one of the new graduate students."

I told him that I was.

He asked all sorts of questions. Where did I come from? Why had I come to Wisconsin? Did I have relatives here? Had I known Professor Meloche? Did I know that the professor was just recently married?

"Had anything to eat?" he finally asked.

I told him I wasn't hungry.

"Nonsense," he said. "Come and share my sandwiches. It'll be an hour or more before he gets back."

It was like an oasis on the desert. Little did I know at that time just how frequent and relaxing my conversations with Ralph in the storeroom would be.

We were still talking when the odor of a cigar drifted into the room. "Smell that?" asked Ralph.

I nodded.

"He's back."

I followed the odor into Professor Meloche's office. He turned around as he heard me come in. A huge cigar drooped from his front teeth, and a large strand of hair hung over his right ear. He sat down at his desk, and in the same motion wound his finger around the misplaced strand of hair.

"Well now, let's see," he said almost in a smile. "Have you seen Professor Holt yet?"

I didn't want to display my ignorance and tell him that I didn't even know who Professor Holt was. "No sir," I replied.

"Well, you've been assigned as one of his teaching assistants. He's been expecting you. Although by now they probably have all the arrangements made for the freshman laboratory. School starts in two days, you know."

Yes I know, I thought. You told me that this morning.

He paused. "Well you'd better report to Professor Holt anyway, just in case there are any last minute preparations for the freshmen that need to be looked after. He'll describe your duties; teaching, quizing, grading papers, and working in the freshman lab. Come back after you've seen him, and in the meantime I'll try to decide where we'll put you."

I looked down at the floor. In my mind were a thousand questions, the most important of which concerned my thesis problem. "I was wondering . . . that is . . . about my thesis."

Professor Meloche looked out the window to hide an expression of disgust, I suspected. "I'm interested in the chemistry of the rare elements, you know, selenium and rhenium," he said. "But we'll find time to talk about that later. Professor Holt's office is on the first floor in that wing." He pointed eastward.

As it turned out, there were a lot of last minute details. Professor Holt put me to work, and I didn't get through until almost four. Professor Meloche's office was locked again, so I wandered down the hall and soon found myself in the library. I went over to the stacks, picked out a reference book, and started to read about rhenium.

I found that rhenium was discovered in 1925 by Walter and Ida Noddack. There were no known rhenium minerals; the element occurred in trace quantities in molybdenite, molybdenum disulfide, an ore occurring in foliated masses or scales looking much like graphite.

To extract molybdenum, the ore is first crushed and then ground. At this stage, the ore is a mixture of many compounds which may include molybdenum sulfide, rhenium sulfide, silica, silicates, and other metal sulfides and oxides. The molybdenum sulfide is concentrated by a flotation process in which a liquid is added to the crushed ore along with a flotation reagent. The flotation reagent forms a film around the particles of molybdenum sulfide and prevents the liquid from wetting the molybdenite. This mixture is then stirred with air, which rises in bubbles, and which forms a froth on the top of the liquid. The molybdenite is caught in the bubbles and is skimmed off with the froth. The silicates, silica, and oxides sink in the liquid and are thus separated from the molybdenite. The concentrated sulfides are first roasted (heated in air) converting the sulfides to oxides:

$$MoS_2 + air \longrightarrow MoO_3 + SO_2$$

Up to this point, rhenium follows molybdenum, but the oxide of rhenium, Re_2O_7, formed on roasting is volatile, so in roasting it evaporates and passes out with the off-gases. Using these principles, the Noddacks produced their first gram of rhenium for about $10,000.

I learned other things about rhenium, too. Re_2O_7 is reduced to the metal with hydrogen. Potassium perrhenate is a white salt which is only slightly soluble in water. In contrast, potassium permanganate is a purple salt which is very soluble. I found an article by Hiskey and Meloche describing a method for determining the amount of rhenium in molybdenum-bearing minerals. The method was based on distillation of perrhenic acid from a concentrated sulfuric acid solution.

I looked up at the clock. It was almost five. I couldn't have been in the library for an hour. I headed back to the professor's office.

"Seen the professor?" I asked Ralph as I passed the storeroom.

He smiled. "Look son," he said, "the professor left for home over an hour ago. Where have you been?"

I could tell from the tone in his voice that Professor Meloche had thought I had been goofing off somewhere.

"Oh," I said as I turned down the hall and headed for home.

The apartment looked just as it had when I left that morning. The bed wasn't made, and suitcases and clothes were still scattered everywhere. Mary wasn't there, and there was no note to tell me where she had gone.

The clock beside the bed stood at 5:25. I looked out the window. Our car was still parked in the street. I went downstairs and asked the landlady if she had seen Mary. She hadn't been around all day, the landlady told me.

I went back upstairs and sat down on the edge of the bed, and I started to imagine all sorts of things. We'd been married only a few months. She wouldn't . . . no, she couldn't. Besides she didn't know anyone in Madison. The car wasn't gone, so she . . . But she's been gone all day. The last thing she said when I left was that she would try to get the place straightened up. I plugged in the table radio and turned it on.

Mechanically, I hung up Mary's coat and put a pair of her shoes in the closet, but I really didn't feel much like unpacking. Then I heard footsteps on the stairs.

"Where have you been?" I didn't even say hello.

"You'll never guess." She was smiling.

"I thought . . . oh, never mind," I said.

"I've got a job."

I felt a little guilty, not only for the things I'd thought, but also because she felt so compelled to get a job, even before we were unpacked.

She didn't seem to mind though. She seemed as happy and bubbly as she'd ever been. "Tell me about school," she said. "Bring that box of cans into the kitchen, and I'll fix something to eat while we talk."

I followed her into the kitchen.

"What happened at school? Did you find out what your research problem . . ."

"Nope. I've been assigned as a teaching assistant to Professor Holt in his dumb freshman class."

She stopped and looked straight at me; she knew I was irritated.

"Besides that, I spent most of the day waiting around in the hall in front of his office," I said.

"Meloche's?" she asked.

"You don't pronounce it that way," I said. "It's not oh, it's ah, it rhymes with gosh."

"Oh."

We laughed.

"Now tell me," she insisted, "did he tell you what your thesis problem will be?"

"In a way."

"What do you mean?"

I scratched my head. "Well," I began slowly, "he said he was interested in rhenium and selenium."

"What are they?"

"They're rare elements." I smiled at her. "I thought you took chemistry."

She ignored me. "Well?"

"Selenium is in the sulfur family," I said. "Many of its reactions are similar to those of sulfur. It's a compound of selenium that makes locoweed poisonous."

The mention of poisonous was like waving a red flag. "Locoweed," she said. "You mean there's actually a weed called locoweed? How poisonous?"

I could see trouble brewing, and I tried to change the subject.

"No," she cut in, "answer my question."

"Look . . ."

"Answer it"

I ran my fingers through my hair. "Yes, there is a loco-weed," I said. "It belongs to the pea family. It grows mostly in the plains country. Sometimes it's called rattle-weed because when it's dry the seed pods rattle . . ."

"No, no," she said, "how poisonous?"

I took a deep breath. "Locoed horses or cattle are not able to control their muscles. Most of the time they act dull and stupid, but sometimes they shake their heads violently and rush about. Eventually they die."

"Are all selenium compounds poisonous?"

I looked out the window. "I don't know," I said slowly. "I suppose."

"You're not going to work on . . ."

"Hold on," I cut in. "He hasn't told me what I'm going to be working on."

Every day after that she'd ask me if Professor Meloche had assigned me a research topic. Every day I'd tell her no. One day she asked another question, "Professor Lewis at Utah gave you a choice for your Master's thesis. Do you think Professor Meloche will?"

I soon found out. As I was walking past his office, I noticed that the professor's door was open and he was sitting at his desk. He looked up over the top of his glasses.

For the first time, I got a good look at Professor Meloche. He was a big man, with long thin black hair that served as his toy. As he opened his mouth to speak, half a cigar almost fell from his lips. "Well?"

I guess I took a long time to say something, because he repeated himself.

"It's about my thesis."

He leaned back in his chair. "Yes," he said, "a thesis topic. Well now let's see." He paused. "I've been wondering." He paused again. "You remember how carbon monoxide was used in the last war as a poison gas?"

I nodded, and at the same time wondered how he expected me to remember that. I was only a few months old when the war ended.

"I ran across a paper the other day," he went on, "that gave me an idea. Manganese dioxide is a good catalyst for the oxidation of carbon monoxide. They use it in gas masks, you know. Anyway, since re-reading the article I've been wondering if some of the rhenium compounds might not be catalysts, too."

I don't know what kind of mental picture the professor had, but I sure know what occurred to me. A simple experiment. A really simple experiment. To test for catalytic activity one would pass a mixture of air and carbon monoxide over the compound under test and then pass the gas stream into lime water to see if a precipitate of calcium carbonate formed:

$$2CO + O_2 \longrightarrow 2CO_2$$

$$Ca(OH)_2 + CO_2 \longrightarrow CaCO_3 + H_2O$$

How extremely simple. A high school problem.

I don't know whether I showed it, but I was annoyed. What a juvenile suggestion, I thought. How could I ever hope that the committee would accept that kind of research for a Ph.D. thesis.

That night I told Mary about it.

"Know what?" I asked. "He wants me to find out if any of the compounds of rhenium are catalysts for the oxidation of carbon monoxide. The Germans used carbon monoxide as a poison gas during the first war and . . ."

"And he thinks they might do it again. Sounds sensible. Sounds like a good topic." She smiled at me.

"Look," I said, "it's a stupid little project, and nobody would give you a Ph.D. for that. I think he's just putting me off."

She smiled at me. "At least you're not working on selenium."

I tromped into the other room. She followed me. "So what are you going to do?" she asked.

"It's slave labor, I tell you. He'll give me a mess of little research projects as they did Claude. I bet I'll be here a year before he really gives me a topic that . . ."

She sat down on the sofa and pulled me down beside her. "Now stop fussing," she said. "Maybe you can talk him out of it. Maybe he doesn't have any other ideas. Or maybe he wants you to get your own ideas."

Perhaps she was right. From what I'd heard around the university, Professor Meloche didn't seem to be the kind that was publication crazy, the kind that went in for what graduate students privately called slave labor. He surely didn't seem to be the kind that would keep you on forever.

If this was the only idea he had, I was presented with an entirely different problem. How do you tell your major professor that you don't like the topic he has assigned you for research? How do you tell him, in truth, that you think his idea is silly? How could I find out if it was a game that he was playing? And where could I get an idea of my own?

But at least I felt I could relax about the slave labor problem. Professor Meloche would not impose what the graduate students called unreasonable research demands for a thesis. I wondered which was worse; no ideas for research or a slave driver. But I did not wonder long. I knew I was lucky to get a major professor who was reasonable and I was glad.

Chapter 2

Seminar

All graduate students in chemistry at Wisconsin were required to take seminar. The seminar for the analytical chemistry students met each Wednesday at 11 a.m. Students were required to take turns giving a one-hour discussion on a topic of general interest in analytical chemistry.

There were so many students in organic chemistry that your turn to speak came up only once a year, but in analytical chemistry we had only 11 students, so our turns came up much more often. Because of the small registration, it was almost a month after school started that we had our first analytical chemistry seminar.

In one of these first seminars, a student named Jim discussed chromatography. If I had known that that would eventually be my thesis subject, I would have listened more carefully and taken notes.

I've often wondered if Jim had relatives in the movie business, because he certainly made a flashy beginning to his talk. He came into the room carrying a long glass tube half filled with a slurry of powdered chalk in water (Figure 1) and two flasks, one containing a green solution and the other a colorless solution. At the sound of the bell, without saying a word, he opened a stopcock at the bottom of the vertical tube and simultaneously poured the colored solution into the top of the tube. The chalk at the top took on a uniform green color (Figure 2) and, to my surprise, the liquid effluent from the bottom of the tube was colorless. Then he poured the colorless solu-

11

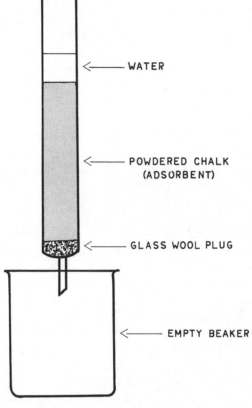

Fig. 1. A chromatographic adsorption column, consisting of powdered chalk in a glass tube

tion into the tube. The green zone started to move but not uniformly. A faint blue zone appeared at the top, and a yellow zone appeared at the bottom of the colored band. He poured in more colorless solution. The blue and yellow bands became larger and larger, and gradually the green zone in the middle disappeared completely, leaving a pure blue zone near the top and a yellow zone midway down in the column (Figure 3).

"That, gentlemen," said Jim, "is chromatography."

Without explaining what had happened, Jim continued his discussion with a review of the history of the subject. In the manufacture of dyes, even in the earliest times, color was tested by placing a drop of solution containing dye on a piece of paper or cloth. Shades of color were obtained by mixing dyes of different colors. The early

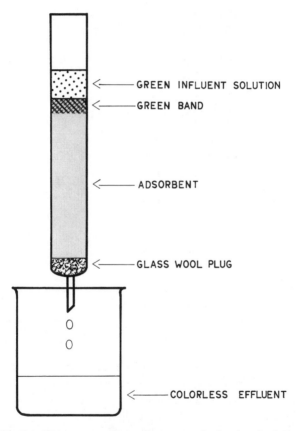

Fig. 2. Chromatographic column on which a band of dyes has been adsorbed. (Dark layer at the top of the column.)

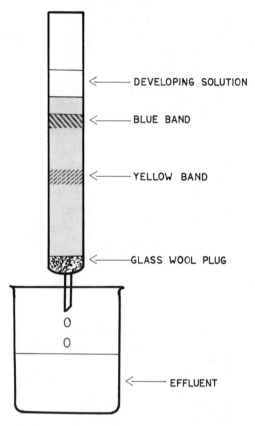

Fig. 3.   Chromatographic column after development, showing two bands. When pure solvent is poured through the column, the band at the top moves more slowly than the one below.

manufacturers noticed that when blends were tested, concentric rings of different colors were formed.

Jim drew a series of concentric rings on the board and shaded them different colors (Figure 4).

Although the users of the test did not know it, they were making a partial chromatographic separation.

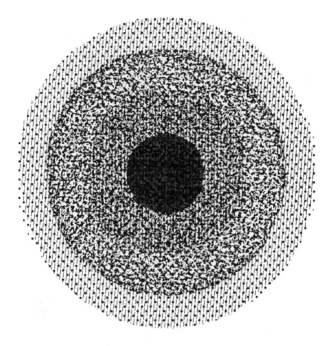

Fig. 4. Runge Rings. When a dye solution is dropped on a piece of paper, the various components of the dye migrate at different rates in the spreading solvent front, resulting in concentric rings of different colors.

Chemists finally came to recognize that, when a drop of liquid is applied to the surface of paper and allowed to spread, materials which are dissolved in the liquid migrate at different rates. In this way mixtures can be resolved, at least partly, into their components. By the turn of the century, many chemists recognized that "capillary analysis," spreading in the capillaries of the paper, could serve as a qualitative analytical tool. However, no one really understood how it worked, and the separation was not complete, *i.e.*, the bands which formed overlapped.

Michael Tswett, a Russian botonist, is generally regarded as the founder or inventor of chromatography because he was the first to really understand the principles and use them in a practical, analytical way.

As is often the case in science, Tswett's method evolved from a rather simple point and grew more complex. In his early experiments, he used simple adsorption on a powder to extract the coloring matter from plants. Later, he extracted by passing the solution containing the colored materials through a stationary column of powder in a glass tube.

In studying the extraction of carotin, the coloring matter in seaweed, Tswett ground the algae with emery and a little calcium carbonate to neutralize the acids using alcoholic petroleum ether as a solvent. During the grinding, the carotin was released from the plant cells and dissolved in the solvent. Tswett repeated the process several times, pouring off the solvent each time, and adding fresh solvent, until no more color was extracted.

His next step was to remove the alcohol, leaving the carotin dissolved in petroleum ether. He did this by shaking the colored extract with water. This mixture he placed in a separatory funnel whereupon the two liquid layers separated, the lower layer being alcohol and water, and the upper layer being petroleum ether and carotin. He discarded the lower layer, but since only part of the alcohol was thus removed, he repeated the process several times until all the alcohol had been extracted. This left him a colored solution of carotin and other colored pigments. To get rid of the undesired pigments, he shook the petroleum ether solution with powdered calcium carbonate. The carbonate adsorbed all the colored pigments except carotin.

Tswett studied the extraction of chlorophyll from higher plants in a similar way, except that he used filter paper pulp to adsorb the pigments. He found that the pigments were adsorbed from petroleum ether solvent whereas alcohol extracted them.

His curiosity led him to try a variety of solid materials as adsorbents. In his experiments he discovered that an adsorbent which is saturated with one dye will sometimes take on another by substitution.

Tswett tried many different approaches. Once he chanced to filter a chlorophyll solution through a column of calcium carbonate in a glass tube. To his surprise, a series of colored zones formed from the top to the bottom of the column.

This discovery led to a frenzy of new experiments in which he found that the dye which was most strongly adsorbed remained at the top of the column, while those which were less strongly adsorbed were picked up in zones lower down in the column.

He then made another observation. If now some pure solvent were poured through the column, the colored bands moved slowly down the column, and the bands or zones which originally overlapped now separated into distinct zones. Tswett called the separate zones in the column a chromatogram and the method chromatography.

Jim drew two pictures on the blackboard using colored chalk, one showing a column with overlapping bands (Figure 5) and the other showing a developed column with separated bands (Figure 6).

I yawned and looked around the room. I wondered if the other students felt as lost as I did. As Jim was saying it, it seemed to make sense, yet I was not sure that I really understood what the words meant, and besides, all that talk about history seemed so unnecessary. I looked at Professor Meloche. He seemed to be fascinated. So did Professor Hall. Our seminars at Utah where I had finished a Master's degree seemed minor league by comparison. I tried to remember what we had studied about adsorption in a colloidal chemistry class there, but the

Fig. 5. An undeveloped chromatogram with overlapping bands

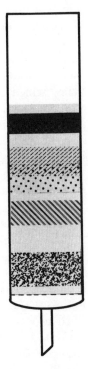

Fig. 6. A developed chromatogram with separated bands

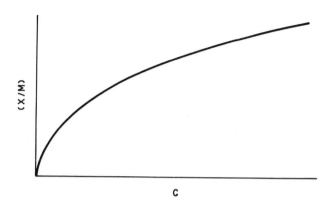

Fig. 7.   Adsorption isotherm characteristic of the adsorption of a solute on a solid. X represents the weight of solute in grams adsorbed on M grams of adsorbent. Hence X/M is the "concentration" of solute in the solid phase, i.e., on the adsorbent. C is the concentration of solute in the solution.

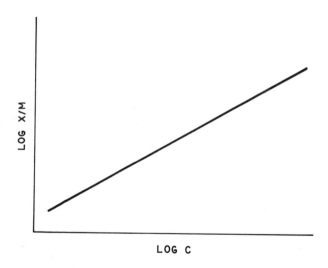

Fig. 8.   Adsorption isotherm plotted on a logarithmic scale

whole thing seemed so far in the past that I could not really remember any of it clearly. I wondered what kind of topic I could discuss when it was my turn at the seminar.

"What are the principles on which the separation is based?" asked Professor Meloche.

Jim walked over to the blackboard, erased the picture of the chromatogram, and drew a graph in its place (Figure 7), a typical Freundlich adsorption isotherm. He drew the same graph on a logarithmic scale (Figure 8). Then he went on to explain that if a solution of sugar and water were stirred with charcoal, the sugar would be adsorbed by the charcoal.

We had studied adsorption in colloidal chemistry, and it was coming back to me. A solution is made up of a solvent (in this case, water) and a solute (in this case, sugar). Things like charcoal which are insoluble in the solvent and which will adsorb solutes from a solution are called adsorbents. Adsorbents have active sites which are capable of attracting and holding solute molecules. Adsorption is a dynamic process; rarely are all the active sites saturated with adsorbed solute (sugar) molecules and rarely are all the solute molecules adsorbed leaving no solute molecules in solution.

Jim explained that isotherms are determined experimentally by shaking a solution with an adsorbent until an equilibrium has been reached and then measuring the concentration of the solute in each phase, *i.e.*, in the solution and on the adsorbent. By repeating this process with several solutions of different concentrations, one is able to measure several equilibrium relationships, and with these several data points, one can plot the isotherm on normal coordinates (Figure 7) or on a logarithmic scale and get a straight line (Figure 8).

I thought of the sugar–water–charcoal example. One could make up several solutions of sugar in water, say 5%,

10%, 15%, and 20%. One could shake 100 ml of the 5% solution with 10 grams of charcoal, allow the adsorption to come to equilibrium, filter off the solid charcoal, and analyze the remaining solution to see how much sugar was left in solution. By difference, one could estimate how much sugar was adsorbed. One could repeat the process with each of the remaining solutions, in turn, and thus determine four adsorption values for sugar on charcoal from water. From this data one could plot an isotherm. I was just beginning to catch up to Jim in my mind when he took off again, with an explanation of adsorption in a column.

Jim noted that when a solution containing a single solute is stirred with an adsorbent, an equilibrium is reached in which the solute partitions or distributes itself partly in the solvent and partly on the adsorbent. On the other hand, if a solution containing a single solute is poured through a stationary column of adsorbent, the solute will be adsorbed on the top layer of the column, and the liquid leaving this layer will be partly depleted in solution. As the solution continues through the column, the concentration of the solute in the solution becomes less and less until it finally reaches zero. In this way a band of solute adsorbed on the adsorbent is found at the top of the column.

If now pure solvent is poured slowly through this column, desorption takes place, and the solvent picks up adsorbed solute until it becomes saturated. If the band extends only part way through the column, the solution containing the desorbed solute continues through the band in the column until it reaches a point at which the adsorbent has unsaturated capacity, at which point the desorbed solute is readsorbed.

By continuing to pour solvent through the column, one can force the adsorbed band to move through the column until it percolates out the bottom. This process of movement of a chromatographic band through a column is called development.

The extent of adsorption of a solute and the rate of movement of a band during development of a chromatogram are determined by (a) the rate at which the solution percolates through the column and (b) the tenacity of adsorption of a solute on the adsorbent. If two solutes differ in their tendency to be adsorbed, the two solutes will move through the column at different rates.

Now consider the case of a solution containing two solutes which is being passed through a column, for example the solution containing the blue and yellow dyes. Jim pointed to the experiment that he had run a few minutes before. In that case, the two dyes competed for adsorption. The relative amount of each dye which was adsorbed was determined by the tenacity of adsorption of each dye, respectively. At first, two overlapping bands were formed, and the column looked green at the top. With the addition of fresh solvent the yellow dye moved more rapidly down the column because it was not as strongly adsorbed. Eventually the two bands were completely separated.

My daydream was cut short by a noise at the front of the room. Jim was displaying a chart summarizing some of the factors which can be varied in chromatographic techniques (*see* Table 1).

Professor Meloche smiled as Jim took down the chart. "Now tell us," he said, "about the process called partition chromatography,"

I squirmed. I wondered if Jim knew the answer. He didn't seem to be the least bit concerned.

"What I've described so far," he went on, "is mostly concerned with adsorption chromatography. By a slight variation in technique, the method can be altered to a process which the professor has mentioned, known as partition chromatography."

Table 1. Variables in Chromatographic Analysis

Nature of the solvent
  water (pH can be varied)
  alcohols
  ethers, petrol ether
  acetone
  benzene
  organic acids (acetic, etc.)
  carbon disulfide

Nature of adsorbent
  inorganic solids:
    silica
    alumina
    magnesia
    zeolites

  organic solids including ion-exchange resins:
    cationic
    anionic

Pre-treatment of adsorbent—effect on adsorption sites
Temperature
Rate of flow through column

Jim scratched his head. "Suppose instead of a solid, one used a stationary liquid?"

"How?" interjected a student from the back of the room.

"By supporting a liquid on a solid; for example, by shaking a solid with a small amount of a liquid, so that a thin film of liquid spreads over the solid making a column of such a combination and passing a solution through said column. The substances being separated distribute themselves between the mobile liquid (solvent) and the stationary one (on the solid). The stationary liquid phase is often water which is bound to silica gel. However, the stationary phase may be an organic solvent which is either more polar or less polar than the mobile phase. Because the materials being adsorbed distribute or partition themselves between the mobile and stationary liquid, the process is called partition chromatography."

Jim paused, and I looked up at the clock. The period was half over.

I reached to feel my wallet in my back pocket. It was still there. It was pay day at the university and I had 90 dollars in my wallet. Mary and I were going to meet at the school cafeteria for a real lunch, the first real lunch in a month.

Daydreaming about lunch was shattered when Jim asked, "Does that answer your question, professor?"

Professor Meloche smiled and nodded.

Jim walked over behind the desk and looked at the chromatogram that he had formed at the beginning of the class. "Let me review what we have covered so far," he said. "Because the experiments of Tswett involved colored compounds, the technique was named chromatography, and we still use this name even though many of the compounds separated by the process are colorless. A chromatogram is the separated bands of pigment in a column. The separation of bands, which occurs by moving the weakly adsorbed compounds through the column more rapidly, we call development. Extraction of the adsorbed material from the column we call elution.

"Initially Tswett depended on the fact that pigments would distribute themselves between a stationary solid adsorbent and a mobile liquid phase. In the meantime, the science of chromatography has advanced so that today chromatography includes a method of separating substances depending on their partition between two immiscible phases. One phase is stationary and the other phase is mobile. The stationary phase tends to retard the movement of the substances to be separated, and the mobile phase tends to carry the substances away. Different substances partition between the stationary and mobile phase in different proportions; those substances which tend to be held by the stationary phase move slowly and those which remain in the mobile phase move rapidly. These differences in the relative rates of movement are the basis for separation in chromatography."

Jim then walked over to the blackboard to summarize the kinds of stationary and mobile phases used in chromatography:

stationary phase		*mobile phase*
solid	—	liquid chromatography
liquid	—	liquid chromatography
liquid	—	gas chromatography

"Tswett's column work and ion-exchange are examples of column, solid–liquid chromatography. In liquid–liquid chromatography, the stationary phase is most often water, and the mobile phase is an organic solvent only slightly miscible with water. Silica gel, which often contains up to 40% bound water, can be used as a support to hold the water. Cellulose can also be used. However, in liquid–liquid partition chromatography, the stationary phase is not limited to water; any liquid spread or adsorbed on the surface of a solid support can be used as the stationary phase. Also, the solid phase is often a powder, but it does not have to be since the combination of a liquid spread on the inside of a long thin tube can also be used, particularly in gas–liquid chromatography. In gas–liquid chromatography, the liquid is, once again, held on a solid support, and the substances to be separated are carried through the column by a carrier gas."

I leaned over to whisper to Harold, a second year graduate student, who was seated next to me, "Man, this guy is covering a lot of stuff. Will we have an exam in seminar? Do they expect us to remember all this?"

Harold smiled, and I could tell that inside he was laughing at me. "No," he said, "there is no exam in seminar, but they might ask you about chromatography during your thesis defense."

I looked at him again, and he was still smiling, and I was not sure whether to believe him or not. Anyway, I thought to myself, by the time I am defending my thesis in two or three years, all the professors will have forgotten about this seminar. Master of all trades, I thought, these professors expect us to be masters of all trades. That is not right, I thought, it is jack of all trades and master of none. I was confused, and yet I was determined to try to follow Jim, just in case Harold was right. I thought of my friend, Tracy, who had flunked out of graduate school, and I was beginning to have a little more empathy for him. My mind was brought back to reality when Jim walked over to the desk and dropped a beaker.

Jim was demonstrating paper chromatography. He cut a piece of filter paper about three quarters of an inch wide and about 10 inches long. Near one end of the paper he dropped a spot of purple food dye. He then took a large test tube and poured into it a small amount of brine solution. He had a cork stopper, cut in half. He put the filter paper between the halves and inserted the stopper into the test tube so that the very end of the paper strip was just below the surface of the liquid. The spot of food dye was about a half inch above the surface of the liquid. As the liquid rose in the capillary pores in the paper, it passed through the dye. Slowly the spot began to move. A blue band began to appear near the top and a red band at the bottom. As the bands moved, the blue eventually became separated from the red, but both bands tailed and spread.

Jim described what had happened: the dye was a mixture of two compounds, one blue and one red, dissolved in a liquid. When the dye was spotted on paper and one end of the paper was dipped into a solvent, the solvent flowed through the paper by capillary action. When the solvent reached the spot, the components of the spot began to move with the solvent at different rates. At the backward edge, where fresh solvent was contacting the spot, the components went into solution and followed the moving phase—the least strongly adsorbed, the blue dye, being picked up by the solvent to the greatest extent. As the solvent passed through the spot, it picked up more blue than red. Eventually the solvent, containing blue and red dyes, reached the forward edge of the spot. At this point adsorption took place. As solvent continued to flow through the spot, this desorption at the trailing edge and adsorption at the leading edge continued. Eventually the spot was washed away. Both the blue and red dye migrated in the direction of flow of the solvent at different rates, the blue dye moving more rapidly until the colors were completely separated (Figure 9).

"In paper chromatography," he went on, "the solvent reservoir must be large enough to contain sufficient liquid to develop the chromatogram and separate the bands. The paper should be suspended free of other objects including the sides of the container, the temperature should be relatively constant, and the vapor phase should be saturated with solvent so that evaporation is minimized.

"Thin film chromatography is, in a way, like paper chromatography. It, too, has two advantages over columns, namely, very small samples are sufficient, and it can be used for two-way resolution—first in one direction and then in another at right angles. One of the disadvantages of thin films is the delicate care needed to handle layers of loose powder.

"Films are usually prepared by spreading a layer of adsorbent powder (and binder if desired) on a glass plate. The uniformity of the thickness of the film is important to avoid three-dimensional effects. A spreader is used to deposit a uniform film (Figure 10).

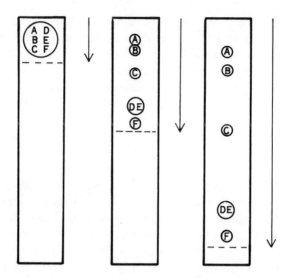

Fig. 9. Example of paper chromatography. Three stages in the separation of a six-component mixture. Stage 1 shows the spot where the original mixture was applied to the paper strip. The arrow on the right and the dotted line show the extent of travel on the solvent front. Stage 2 shows the separation of the components after partial development. Stage 3 shows the chromatogram after further development. Note that in the case of components A and B the separation is poor, and components D and E remain together.

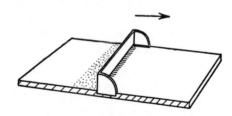

Mikrochimica Acta

Fig. 10. A spreader for depositing a thin adsorbent film on a glass plate (*1*)

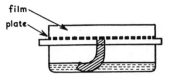

Fig. 11. Apparatus for development of a thin film chromatograph. Developing solution is fed to the film by a cotton wick through a hole drilled in the glass plate which supports thin (adsorbent) film (2).

"Among the adsorbents which can be used in thin film chromatography are alumina, silica, magnesia, powdered ion-exchange resins, powdered polyethylene, and powdered cellulose.

"A requirement for a good chromatogram is that the spot be as small as possible. This can be accomplished using a micropipette or micrometer syringe. The solvent in the drop should evaporate rapidly.

"If the film is about 250 microns thick, about 10 micrograms of sample is about right for linear development and about 200 micrograms for circular or radial development. Solutions are usually about 1–2%."

Jim added that the chromatogram is developed by feeding solvent through the film. If the film is a loose powder it is usually held horizontally (Figure 11), but if it contains binder it can be developed at any angle (Figure 12). Examples of chromatograms developed linearly and radially are shown in Figure 13.

Table 2. Thin Film Chromatography

Factors Influencing Rate and Development

Solvent
Thickness of adsorbent film
Particle size of adsorbent
Angle of the chromato plate
Atmosphere surrounding the plate

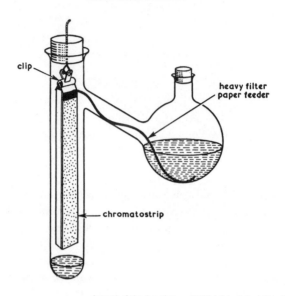

Fig. 12. Apparatus for developing a thin film which contains a binder. The plate is hung vertically, and the developing solution percolates through it (3).

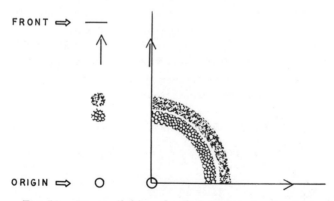

Fig. 13. Linear (left) and radial (right) development of the same mixture

Jim then displayed a second table (Table 2) summarizing some of the factors which influence the rate of development in thin film chromatography.

Harold poked me. I leaned over so he could whisper in my ear. "It's all pretty simple, isn't it? It all works the same way," he said.

I suspected that he was leading me on, but I could not be sure from the expression on his face. "What do you mean by that?" I asked.

"Well, if you want to separate two things, you just pick a stationary phase which tends to pick up one of the things more strongly than the other. That's really all there is to it." He smiled at me.

I disagreed. "In the first place it is not that simple. And besides, there are a lot of different kinds of stationary phases and moving phases and a lot of ways of arranging things—like films or columns.

"Now come on," Harold chided. "The principle is the same in every case. You have a solute. It tends to go partly in one phase and partly in another, but because there is a moving phase, it tends to be swept out. You have another solute which is held by the stationary phase, either more or less strongly, so it moves out at a faster or slower rate. What could be more simple than that? It is like two swimmers, swimming downstream. One swims faster than the other, because someone has hold of the swimsuit of the slower swimmer. So one swimmer gets to the finish before the other one."

I thought to myself, thanks a lot. I looked up just in time to see Jim looking at the clock. Maybe it is not that complicated, I thought, but I wish he'd hurry and get through so I could go to lunch.

I looked up; Jim was still looking at the clock, almost as if in a trance. I wondered if he had forgotten what he was going to say. There were about 10 minutes left in the period. I sensed a pained expression on his face.

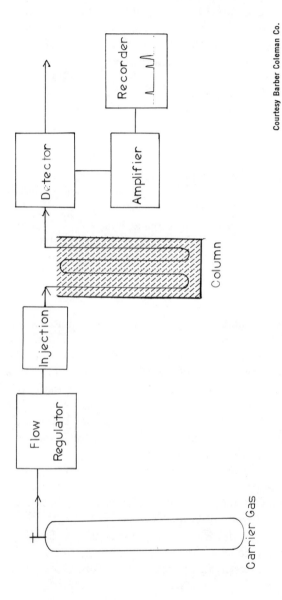

Fig. 14. Apparatus used in gas chromatgraphy

Maybe he just had lots more to say. "Let's return, for a moment," he said, "and talk a little more about gas chromatography. As I have already mentioned, it is possible to use a gas as the mobile phase, and a nonvolatile liquid as the stationary phase. The nonvolatile liquid can be supported on an inert solid, on the internal surface of a capillary tube or on an active solid."

Jim further explained that in gas chromatography, the components to be separated are carried in a gas stream. The basic apparatus for gas chromatography is shown in Figure 14. The advantages of gas chromatography lie in the low viscosity of the mobile phase and the high diffusion rates of gases. Jim went on talking but I was not really listening. All I could do was think of that money in my pocket. I came back to the real world when Jim showed a typical gas chromatogram, Figure 15.

"By now," Jim continued, "it is evident that there are many variations in the chromatographic technique. A salt mixture can be sent through a support coated with a precipitating agent. Electrochromatography is a process in which ions are carried through a column or sheet under the influence of an electric field. Chromatography can be combined with electrophoresis. Papers can be impregnated with solids like silica or alumina, and of course, ion-exchange chromatography done with synthetic ion exchange resins."

Jim looked up at the clock. "There is not time," he said, "to discuss the theoretical aspects of chromatography in detail, but let me say just this: behavior of a substance moving in a column is affected not only by the constants in the isotherm (equilibrium), but also by the rate at which the solvent passes through the column (kinetics). In addition, the theoretical considerations include the forces between the substances to be separated and the stationary phases including any supporting medium. These forces can vary in strength from ordinary chemical

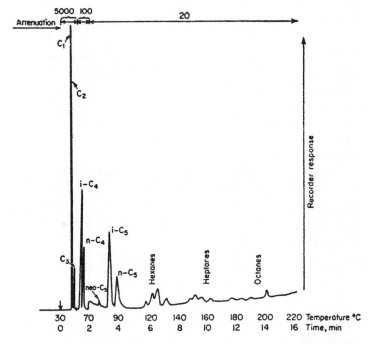

Gas Chromatography

Fig. 15. Separation of the components of natural gas by gas chromatography. The column was packed with glass beads treated with fibrous alumina and colloidal silica (*see* Fig. 32). Natural gas is mostly methane (CH_4), but it also contains small amounts of higher hydrocarbons (ethane C_2H_6, propane C_3H_8, *n*-butane, C_4H_{10}, isobutane, etc.) (*4*).

bonds, to hydrogen bonds, to relatively weak physical attractions (van der Waals forces). The size of the ion or molecule to be adsorbed is likewise a consideration, particularly if there is some physical limitation with regard to the size or shape of the site on which adsorption can take place (steric hindrance)."

The bell rang. The seminar was over.

CHAPTER 3

Thesis Assignment?

The seminar on chromatography was constantly on my mind. I guess it was partly because I wished I had a thesis assignment like that and partly because I was so dissatisfied with my topic. But time, as it so often does, eventually stifled my thoughts of chromatography, and my attention focused on the problems of getting started on my assigned research.

One of the first things I did was to review the literature pertinent to my assigned topic. I must admit that I did not go into this task with much enthusiasm, mostly because of my negative attitude toward the assignment. However, eventually my conscience allowed me no more peace, and I forced myself to spend several afternoons in the chemistry library at the university.

Initially, I read mostly about the chemistry of rhenium, but eventually I included articles on the catalytic oxidation of carbon monoxide.

It was then that I found an article on "The Physical Chemistry of Hopcalite Catalysts," by Pitzer and Frazer of the department of chemistry at Johns Hopkins University. They had undertaken their study to explore the mechanism of the reaction and the needs for a catalyst.

The paper reporting their findings contained a theoretical section, and it was in this section that I found the information which eventually released me from the research topic I had been assigned. Among the characteristics of an oxide which are desirable for catalytic activity, Pitzer and Frazer listed fineness of subdivision. They stated that, to be catalytically active, the material should be precipitated and dried under conditions that would retard crystal growth. In the case of manganese dioxide catalysts, the scientists reported that the catalyst particles were so small that their diameter probably ran no more than 10 unit cells. The same was true of other catalysts such as cupric oxide and cobalt oxide; in a crystallographic study of these materials the researchers found that the crystal planes were very poorly developed. But their studies indicated that fineness of subdivision is not the only criterion for catalytic activity.

Their experiments on reaction mechanism led to the conclusion that catalysis occurred by adsorption of the carbon monoxide by the catalyst, that a bond was formed between the catalyst and carbon monoxide, followed by splitting out of carbon dioxide. They concluded the catalyst undergoes alternate reduction and oxidation, and only those oxides should be catalytic for which the reaction

$$MO_x + CO \longrightarrow MO_{x-1} + CO_2$$

proceeds with a decrease of free energy. They found that the number of oxides obeying this criterion far exceeds the number of oxides which are catalytic. They concluded that fineness of subdivision and an oxide which is thermodynamically unstable in the presence of carbon monoxide are not sufficient conditions for catalytic activity.

The additional key to catalysis was the geometric match of the carbon monoxide structure to that of the catalyst. In the active catalysts—manganese dioxide, nickelic oxide, and cobaltic oxide—the metal-to-oxygen distance lies in the narrow range between 1.75 and 1.85 Angstroms. Of the many materials they investigated, none which had interatomic distances outside this range were catalytic at room temperature.

Pitzer and Frazer concluded that to be catalytic an oxide must be finely divided, it must satisfy the criterion of favorable free energy change for the reduction of the oxide by carbon monoxide, and it must have an interatomic distance in the range of 1.75 to 1.85 Angstroms.

I finished reading the article, leaned back in my chair, and gazed out the library window. It was one of those fall days when the air is crisp and cool, and the sky is filled with billowy white clouds. A grin crossed my face. I felt much like the weather outside, or like a young colt on an autumn day, kicking his heels in the air and dashing around the pasture.

There was really no point in investigating the catalytic activity of rhenium compounds, for I knew even without looking it up that the rhenium–oxide interatomic distance was much larger than the 1.75–1.85 Angstroms required. I made some notes in my research notebook, dated them, and went outside to think things over.

Only one problem remained: how to convince Professor Meloche that there was no point in studying catalytic activity of rhenium oxide for the oxidation of carbon monoxide.

My chance came a few days later. I was in my research laboratory, studying for an exam in advanced inorganic chemistry when the professor walked in. From the way he started the conversation, and the questions he asked, I could tell that his only objective in coming to see me was that of being friendly. He asked if my wife and I were adjusting to Wisconsin, if we had found a satisfactory apartment, if Mary had found a job, and all sorts of similar questions. But not once did he bring up the topic of my research. The more we talked, the more I wiggled about on my chair, and finally I decided that if this conversation were going to include my research project, I would have to bring it up myself.

I took a deep breath and looked out the windows. "I read an article the other day," I said. I paused and scratched my head. "It was about hopcalite catalysts."

He didn't reply. He didn't even move. I wondered what he was thinking, I wondered if he was listening. There was a long period of silence. Finally he said, "Oh. Anything of interest?"

I cleared my throat. "I think so." I watched a cloud form over the trees. "The authors found that there were several essential criteria for a material to be catalytically active for the oxidation of carbon monoxide at room temperature." I paused to see whether he would have any reaction. The pause became long and uncomfortable.

"Well," he said at length, "what were they?"

"One was that the free energy for the reduction of the oxide by carbon monoxide must be favorable," I said.

"Well, the oxides of rhenium are certainly easily reduced." The professor smiled, walked over toward the laboratory hood, and looked in.

"Another requirement," I said, "is that the metal-to-oxygen interatomic distance of the oxide must be in the range of 1.75 to 1.85 Angstroms."

Again there was a long period of silence. Finally the professor turned and looked directly at me. "I see," he said. "I guess that means you'll have to find yourself a new research topic." There was another long pause, and then he added, "Do you have any ideas?" He smiled and walked out the door.

I felt elated and deflated all at the same time. I was elated because I knew that the professor really didn't care what I had for a thesis project. He had only suggested the catalytic oxidation of carbon monoxide by rhenium compounds to get me started on something, but what really concerned me was how could I ever find an idea for a research problem which would be acceptable to the faculty of the chemistry department of the University of Wisconsin. I had always wanted to select my own research project, but now that the opportunity had come, I was not the least bit sure of myself.

Days came and went. Then weeks, then months. I became so involved with studying for qualifying examinations that I thought about little else, least of all my thesis.

The university chemistry department gave four qualifying examinations in chemistry. All Ph.D. candidates had to take three of the four, any three of their choice. These examinations were given once a year. Ph.D. candidates were expected to take these during their first year in graduate school. The year that I was there, the exams were given in May. As the month approached, I worried more and more. I heard stories of other fellows who had failed their examinations, and knew they had been invited to leave. I sure didn't want that to happen to me. So every moment that I had, I studied for the qualifiers.

Mary became bored. Fortunately she was working at a drug store near the university, and this kept her occupied much of the time, but our apartment was small and there was little to do in the evening. She wanted to talk or do other things when I wanted to study.

I remember one Sunday afternoon, I went to the university to study because it would be quiet there, no interruptions. But it was so deathly quiet that after an hour I came home, only to find that Mary had gone off with some friends. I was furious. I guess I expected her to be there, sort of like a picture on the wall.

A few days later, Mary announced that the landlady, Mrs. Clayton, had told us we were going to have to move.

"It can't be true. It just can't be true, I don't believe it."

Mary went right on fixing dinner. "But it is," she said, "it is."

We debated for several minutes, and finally she told me to go down and ask Mrs. Clayton myself. I'll never forget Mary—sitting on the steps, giggling as I came back embarrassed because Mrs. Clayton did not have any idea what I was talking about.

May finally arrived, and with it, the dreaded qualifying exams. The day I heard that I had passed them was a wonderful day. I remember how relieved I was, and yet not completely relieved because all the time I'd been studying for the qualifiers I'd completely neglected my thesis.

I still didn't have any idea for a research topic, so to fill the void I decided to spend my research time helping a couple of my colleagues who were working on a government-sponsored research project on rhenium.

Following the discovery of rhenium, many scientists attempted to extract that element from natural products. For years, Germany produced the world's supply, but as a result of the war, the supply to the United States was cut off. It therefore became necessary to find an alternate source of supply to satisfy commercial demands. The problem was difficult because no characteristic rhenium mineral had ever been found. Furthermore, in minerals that contain rhenium, only trace amounts of that element are present.

Rhenium occurs as a minor constituent in molybdenite, MoS_2. In extracting molybdenum from molybdenite, rhenium is concentrated along with the molybdenum. When the ore is floated, rhenium follows molybdenum. The sulfide concentrate is placed in a furnace and heated while a stream of air is passed over it. This is called roasting. During roasting, molybdenite reacts with the oxygen of the air to form molybdenum trioxide:

$$2 \ MoS_2 + 7 \ O_2 \longrightarrow 2 \ MoO_3 + 4 \ SO_2$$

By a similar reaction, rhenium sulfide is oxidized to rhenium heptoxide, Re_2O_7. Rhenium heptoxide is volatile. As a result it tends to pass out of the furnace with the exit gases. As these gases pass into the cooler flues, the rhenium heptoxide is condensed and deposits in the flues along with other fine dusts which have been carried out of the furnace by the gases. In this way, from a molybdenite ore which may contain only a few parts per million of rhenium, a flue dust is obtained which contains as much as 1% rhenium. The major constituents of the flue dust are molybdenum oxide and selenium oxide.

Two of my colleages at the University of Wisconsin were studying a fractional sublimation method for recovering rhenium heptoxide from molybdenite flue dust. They reasoned that because rhenium heptoxide was more volatile than the molybdenum trioxide, a separation of rhenium from the flue dust should be possible by a controlled temperature roasting.

In their studies they recovered only about 19% of the rhenium. We wondered why. Our discussions of the problem led us to believe that there were several possible reasons: molybdenite flue dust contains some basic or alkaline constituents, these react with acidic rhenium heptoxide to form salts which are not volatile, and the large amount of MoO_3 present in the concentrate thermally insulates the mass and mechanically retains Re_2O_7. Another problem was the fact that the rhenium heptoxide which was volatilized was very difficult to condense, and much of it escaped. Still another problem was that selenium was concentrated along with rhenium, and these elements had to be separated.

Interesting studies, these, but before I really got involved with them the tempo of the war stepped up, and I left the university to work on the Manhattan project.

CHAPTER 4

Amberlite IR–4B

World War II finally came to a halt with the dropping of atomic bombs, fruits of the Manhattan Project, and Mary and I returned to Madison that September. Except for two classes my course work was completed, and all that remained was a thesis and an examination in my major. The question that was constantly on my mind was what should I have for a research problem.

Several ideas came to mind, but none seemed really suitable. I felt that I should discuss my ideas with someone, at least with Professor Meloche and yet I couldn't bring myself to do it because I really did not have an idea for a research topic that I was completely satisfied with. One day as I went for my mail, I met Professor Matthews of the chemistry department. For some moments he stood in front of his mail box, peering at a small package. Finally he turned to me, handed me the package, and said, "Are you interested?"

I took it and returned to my research laboratory. The package was from the Rohm and Haas Co. of Philadelphia; it contained a small sample of an ion exchange resin, Amberlite IR–4B, along with a brochure. I didn't have anything else to do, so I read the brochure.

Amberlite IR–4B is a weak base, phenol–formaldehyde-type anion exchange resin recommended for acid removal. It has high regeneration efficiency which means that after use its ion exchange activity is readily restored. It is brownish-orange and consists of particles about half a millimeter in diameter. It is shipped in a moist, fully-swollen condition, but it expands 25% during its conversion from the hydroxide to the chloride form. It will extract essentially all anions from water as long as the pH is below 7, *i.e.*, the solution is acidic. It is often used with cation exchange resins to produce deionized water, and when it is, essentially all dissolved salts are removed except silica and carbon dioxide.

Anions can be removed from exhausted or used Amberlite IR–4B by treating it with a dilute solution of sodium carbonate, ammonium hydroxide, or sodium hydroxide. When generating the resin, removing the adsorbed anions, Rohm and Haas recommend that the concentration of regenerate should not exceed 2%. It is best to regenerate the spent or exhausted resin by passing the regenerating solution through a bed (column) of the ion exchange resin slowly.

After the resin has been backwashed and regenerated with the alkaline solution, it is then washed to remove cations. This is done by passing deionized water through the column down flow. Backwash removes only dissolved or small resin particles and reclassifies the resin particles in the bed.

Rohm and Haas recommend that, for normal operation, the mineral acidity of the influent solution should be dilute, *i.e.*, $0.01N$.

The rated capacity of Amberlite IR–4B is 25 kilograins as calcium carbonate per cubic foot. The density of the resin, as shipped, is 35 pounds per cubic foot. Procedures for determining the capacity are detailed in the Appendix.

A cupful of wet Amberlite IR–4B weighs about 150 grams; this amount will adsorb about 300 milliequivalents of negative ions. With hydrochloric acid (HCl) which has a molecular weight and equivalent weight of 36.5, a cupful of resin will adsorb about 10 grams of HCl (300 milliequivalents/cupful) (36.5 grams/equivalent).

One statement in the Rohm and Haas brochure caught my attention: "The capacity of IR–4B for each inorganic and organic acid differs, depending on the ionization constant, the concentration, the equivalent weight, and the degree of hydration of the specific acid involved."

I read the statement again, and while I did I kept thinking about Jim's seminar on chromatography and the time that we had tried to recover rhenium (as the heptaoxide, Re_2O_7) from flue dust concentrate by a controlled temperate roasting. I wondered if Amberlite IR–4B could be used to separate perrhenic and molybdic acids. Would such a topic be satisfactory for a Ph.D. thesis? I sat there for a long time pondering these questions. I wanted to talk with the professor, and at the same time I wanted the thrill of working the problem out by myself. I'd heard stories about how dogmatic some professors had been with their students. I didn't want to get caught in that kind of a trap, a trap where the professor makes suggestions that the student is forced to investigate.

Inwardly, I felt that the professor really would approve of my choice anyway.

I decided to take a chance. I determined that the chromatographic separation of perrhenic and molybdic acids would be the topic of my thesis, and that I would not discuss my plans with the professor or anyone on the staff of the university until the study was underway.

CHAPTER 5

Ion Exchange Chromatography

My first step was to write Rohm and Haas Co. to ask them for a larger sample of Amberlite IR–4B resin and any additional literature pertaining to ion exchange resins and chromatographic separation.

It seemed like years before I got an answer. Actually it was only a week, but when you are as eager as I was, a week can seem like a very long time.

I still remember the big day when the Rohm and Haas reply came. My hands were all sweaty as I tore open the package containing several articles and pamphlets.

The brochure that I read first was "Ion Exchange with Amberlite Resins." Rohm and Haas was the first company in the United States to produce synthetic ion exchange resins commercially. Initially, ion exchange resins were used in water conditioning, but today their uses have expanded, and they serve in the production of pharmaceuticals, to combat the effect of peptic ulcers and cardiac edema, to concentrate and recover precious metals, to catalyze agents in organic chemical reactions, to deionize sugar syrups, and to make possible the separation, isolation, and analysis of a host of compounds or elements too elusive for most conventional chemical techniques.

Many molecules are composed in turn of still smaller particles known as ions. The ions in a crystal are bound together by electrical charges; those which bear a positive charge are called cations and those bearing a negative charge, anions. In table salt (sodium chloride), sodium is the cation and chloride the anion. Salts like sodium chloride ionize in water, *i.e.*, the solid crystals separate into the component ions, and these go their separate ways in the solution.

$$NaCl \longrightarrow Na^+ + Cl^-$$

Years ago, before detergents, soaps were commonly used for cleansing. One of the problems in using soaps is a gummy precipitate that sometimes forms. Most natural waters contain dissolved magnesium and calcium compounds, hence magnesium and calcium cations. Both of these ions react with soaps to form insoluble compounds:

$$Ca^{2+} + 2CH_3(CH_2)_{16}COO^- \longrightarrow Ca(CH_3(CH_2)_{16}COO)_2$$

If water containing dissolved calcium or magnesium compounds, *i.e.*, Ca^{2+} or Mg^{2+}, is used with soap, the reaction occurs. Soft sticky curds in a washing machine and the ring around a bathtub are examples of this reaction.

Sodium ions do not form a precipitate with soap, so if calcium or magesium ions in hard water could be replaced with sodium ions, no precipitate would be formed when the water comes in contact with soap. Not only is the nuisance of the curds or the scale on the bathtub eliminated, but also the soap is not wasted in forming a useless precipitate.

Years ago water was softened by passing it through zeolites, a complex, naturally occurring, aluminum silicate mineral. Today water can be softened with ion exchange resins. During water softening the hard water passes through a column filled with a cation exchange resin. Calcium and magnesium ions in the water react with the ion exchange resin, which exchanges these ions for sodium ions, leaving the water softened (Figure 16).

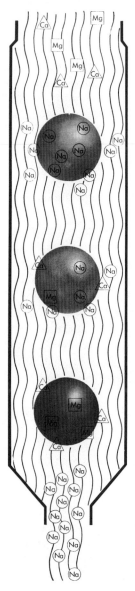

Courtesy Rohm and Haas Co.

Fig. 16. Water softening. Hard water—water containing calcium and magnesium ions—is admitted to the ion exchange column. The resin particles in the column have replaceable sodium cations and fixed, irreplaceable anions. There are, of course, thousands of particles in a typical exchanger unit, each particle containing not just a few ions, but literally billions. The calcium and magnesium ions are adsorbed by the resin which in turn releases sodium ions. Two sodium ions are released for each calcium or magnesium ion. The effluent water is soft, i.e., it does not contain calcium or magnesium cations, the hardness-producing cations. The resin bed may be regenerated by adding to it a solution containing sodium ions, e.g., sodium chloride.

Ion exchange reactions are reversible, and this makes it possible to regenerate the ion exchange column for reuse when the resin is exhausted. In general, cation exchange resin has a greater affinity for one type of ions than another, e.g., a greater affinity for Ca^{2+} than Na^+, but the effect can be overcome in a chromatographic process. In regeneration of a cation exchange resin saturated with calcium ions, a concentrated solution of sodium chloride is passed through the column. By sheer force of numbers, the calcium ions are removed from the resin and replaced by sodium ions. Thus a resin which had been exhausted by hard water is regenerated by passing a concentrated solution of table salt through the column. The resin is then ready for reuse.

The advantages of soft water in the home are many. Heating bills for hot water are reduced because with soft water there is no mineral deposit in the heat exchanger, the hot water heater. For the same reason, plumbing maintenance is reduced. Hair washed in soft water is soft and more lustrous, skin is softer and smoother. When soaps are used, soft water eliminates soap curd formation and saves as much as 50% of the soap which is otherwise precipitated by calcium and magnesium ions. Clothes which are laundered in soft water are softer and have a longer life.

In the research laboratory as well as in industry, it is often desirable to have pure water, water which is free of all ions. Pure water can be prepared by distillation, but this is expensive. Now the job can and frequently is done with ion exchange resins. For example, in hard water the soluble compound is frequently calcium sulfate; hence, in hard water sulfate ions are present along with calcium ions. In other words, some hard waters are a dilute solution of calcium sulfate. Deionized water is prepared from hard water by using a cation exchange resin and an anion exchange resin. If the cation exchange resin has been regenerated with an acid, the magnesium and calcium in hard water are replaced with hydrogen ions as it passes over the cation exchanger. The water emerges from the exchange column as dilute sulfuric acid. If this dilute sulfuric acid is passed through an anion exchange resin which has been regenerated with a hydroxide solution so that the hydroxide group is the mobile anion, the sulfate ions are replaced with hydroxide ions as the dilute sulfuric acid solution comes in contact with this exchange resin. The hydroxide ions react with hydrogen ions to form water, and the water emerging from the unit is ion free (Figure 17).

Some of the industrial uses of ion exchange resins include recovery of: copper from rayon pickling wastes, gold from cyanide leach liquors, zinc from mine waters, chromium from plating baths, rare earth metals from their ores, magnesium from sea water, amino acids from distillers' solutions, meat scraps, byproducts, and fishing wastes, citric and ascorbic acids from citrus wastes, fatty acids from soap wastes, tartaric acids from wine residues, and nicotinic acid from vitamin production wastes.

In one of the booklets I discovered a glossary of ion exchange. I found it useful to read through this glossary because many of the terms in it were used throughout the other booklets. I referred to the glossary often, and it is included at the end of this book.

In another booklet I found a discussion of batch and column techniques. In batch operation, an ion exchange resin is stirred with the solution to be treated. When equilibrium is reached, the treated solution is removed by decantating or filtering, and the resin may be regenerated. For example, if a resin which is saturated with chloride ions is exposed to a solution containing perrhenate ions, an exchange will occur, and some of the

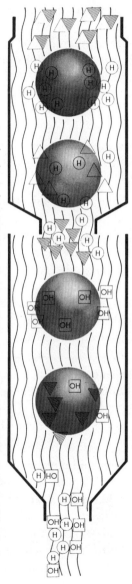

Courtesy Rohm and Haas Co.

Fig. 17. Deionization. A solution containing ionic materials, *i.e.*, soluble salts (the cations are represented in the figure by open triangles and the anions by shaded triangles) is admitted to a column of cation exchange resin which has mobile, replaceable hydrogen ions associated with it. As the solution percolates through the exchanger, the cations in solution are adsorbed onto the resin particles, which in turn release their hydrogen ions. The water leaving the column contains hydrogen ions and the negative groups—anions—originally present in the solution. It is now admitted to a second column of anion exchange resin which has associated with it mobile, replaceable hydroxyl anions. In the anion column the anions in the solution are adsorbed onto the anion exchanger, replacing the hydroxyl ions. The effluent is essentially chemically pure water. (The hydrogen ions combined with the hydroxyl ions to produce water.)

perrhenate will be adsorbed on the resin, leaving the resin partly as chloride and partly as perrhenate.

Amberlite IR–4B resin in the chloride form is expressed chemically as RNH_3Cl, where R– is the organic part of the resin which holds the active sites to the resin, $-NH_3-$ is the active site where adsorption and desorption take place, and –Cl is the adsorbed chloride. Resin in the perrhenate form is written as RNH_3ReO_4. Thus the exchange reaction is written:

$$RNH_3Cl + ReO_4^- \rightleftarrows RNH_3ReO_4 + Cl^-$$

The double arrow means the reaction goes in both directions, establishing an equilibrium in which all four species are present: resin as chloride, resin as perrhenate, chloride ions, and perrhenate ions. Most ion exchange reactions are equilibrium reactions and hence rarely go to completion in a single batch exposure, the exceptions being those cases where there is a strong driving force for the reaction.

Quantitative ion removal can be achieved by using a column. In this case the ion exchange resin is placed in a vertical column, called a bed. The solution which is to be treated is percolated through the bed. An ion exchange column may be regarded as a series of very thin batch operations, somewhat analogous to multiple places for boiling in a distillation column.

Consider the system of an ion exchange column in which the resin is in the chloride form, and a solution of perrhenic acid is percolated through the bed. When an ion exchange resin in the chloride form is stirred with a solution of perrhenic acid, an equilibrium is reached in which there is a mixture of perrhenic and hydrochloric acids in solution, and the resin is partly in the perrhenate and partly in the chloride form. Thus, not all of the resin is converted to the perrhenate form, and its available capacity for perrhenate is not completely utilized. This is what happens in the "first layer" in the ion exchange column.

The solution passing to the "second layer" now contains less perrhenic acid. None of the resin in the second layer is in the perrhenate form; hence a different equilibrium level is established in this part of the column in which additional perrhenic acid is removed from the solution. Now as the solution continues on its way through the bed it becomes more and more depleted of perrhenic acid and contains more and more hydrochloric acid—exchanged for perrhenic. The series of exchanges continues, and if the column is long enough, by the time the solution emerges from the bottom of the column it will be completely devoid of perrhenic acid. For each perrhenate ion in the original solution, the solution will now contain a chloride ion.

I was so engrossed in reading that I didn't hear Mary come into my laboratory. "What are you doing?" she asked.

I looked up. "What am I doing? What are you doing? Did you leave work early?"

She had a disgusted look on her face. "No, I didn't leave work early. As a matter of fact I've been downstairs waiting for you for . . . I don't know how long." She bobbed her head as she often did when she'd run out of patience.

"I didn't realize it was so late. I'm sorry." I paused. "Want to eat at the cafeteria tonight?"

The cafeteria in the student union building was the favorite place for married graduate students when they ate out. The food was inexpensive, good, and plentiful.

"All right," she said with a smile.

The evening was crisp. I took a deep breath as we left the building. It smelled good. "I got the package," I said as we headed down University Avenue.

"What package?"

"The one from Rohm and Haas, about ion exchange resins."

"Oh."

"Is that all you can say, oh?"

She looked at me and smiled again. "What did you want me to say?"

"Nothing, I guess."

"Why did you ask then?"

"It's just that . . ." I paused. "Well . . . I think I've got a thesis topic."

She was watching a squirrel, and I got the impression she wasn't listening. There was a long pause. "Well . . . go on," she said.

"Remember that seminar on chromatography? The one I told you about . . ." I could tell by the expression on her face that she didn't. "You know . . . separating things in columns . . . it was when we first came to Madison."

"But that was three years ago. How do you expect me to remember what happened to you three years ago?"

I decided to start over.

"Do you know what chromatography is?" I asked.

"Not really."

"Well . . . it's a way to separate things."

"Like separating peas from pods?"

"Not exactly." I paused. "Suppose you have a solution of sodium chloride and calcium chloride. If you pour the solution through a chromatographic column, the calcium will be extracted, and the sodium will all come through."

"Come on now, get serious." She smiled again, and wiggled her shoulders which was her way of saying she felt kittenish.

"Remember the old water-softeners we used to have?"

She nodded.

"Well, I just found out why they work."

"What does that have to do with chromato . . . what's it called?"

"It's the same thing. Water-softeners work chromatographically." I explained it to her. "And know what?" I continued. "I think chromatographic ion exchange can be used to separate perrhenic and molybdic acids."

"If it's that easy why didn't you and Harold and Luke do it that way before we left?"

"For one thing," I said, "I didn't have the idea then."

"Oh." She paused and I knew she had something on her mind. "Just what makes you so sure it will work?"

"It has to," I said, "you just pour the mixed solution through a column of anion exchange resin and . . ." I paused.

"And?"

"The ions get separated . . . I guess."

"You guess, don't you know? Which one comes out first? How big a column? Can you get the one that sticks off? Are there any tricks? Need I go on?" She paused and we laughed.

"I guess there are a few details that I haven't worked out yet."

"Well," she replied, "how are you going to go about working them out?"

"Those brochures." I looked up at the sky and watched an airplane cross paths with a bird. "I was reading those brochures from Rohm and Haas when you came. I expect that I'll find some of the answers in them."

"So that's what you were doing. I should have known."

After we ate, she suggested that we go to a movie. I was about to object, by saying that I'd never get through graduate school if we went to movies on school nights, and then I remembered that I'd promised to take her last weekend before I got the book, "Valency." So off we went to the theater.

It wasn't till the next morning when I got back to the laboratory that I was able to finish reading the articles on ion exchange. Among the collection I found a book called "Laboratory Guide." I flipped to the section on Preparation of Laboratory Columns.

For small-scale studies, a laboratory buret can be used to make an ion exchange column. The bed of ion exchange resin is supported in the column by inserting a small plug of glass wool above the stopcock burette. Columns can also be made from glass tubes of various diameters by fusing a sintered glass plate in the tube and drawing the tube down in the bottom section. Chromatographic effects are best achieved by using long columns with relatively small diameters, providing a long thin path with many layers (like stacked poker chips) for ion exchange.

Solution to be added to the column, *i.e.*, the stock solution from which the ions are to be exchanged, and the regenerating solutions, are introduced to the top of the column, for example, from a separatory funnel attached at the top of the column with a rubber stopper (Figure 18). Actually, any convenient vessel can be used as long as the liquid can flow from it into the column. Such reservoirs should be placed higher than the top of the column so that the feed is by gravity. Attachment to the column should be airtight (Figure 19).

I was in the middle of reading the Rohm and Haas Laboratory Guide book on ion exchange when Ralph Helmke, the store room man, came into my laboratory.

"What are you doing?" he asked.

"Reading about ion exchange."

"Oh, what's that?"

I told him and showed him a picture of a laboratory ion-exchange column.

"Looks simple," he said.

"Oh!"

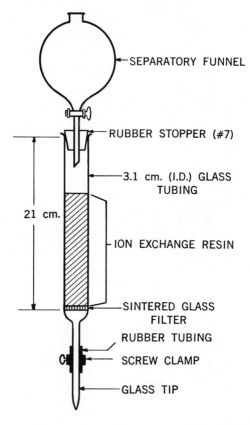

SEPARATORY FUNNEL

RUBBER STOPPER (#7)

3.1 cm. (I.D.) GLASS TUBING

21 cm.

ION EXCHANGE RESIN

SINTERED GLASS FILTER

RUBBER TUBING

SCREW CLAMP

GLASS TIP

Courtesy Rohm and Haas Co.

Fig. 18. An ion exchange column

"What do you mean, oh?"

I did not want to take the time to explain it to him, so I said, "Maybe it is."

"And maybe it isn't," he replied.

I was afraid that the only way I was going to be able to get rid of him was to explain it to him, and I really did not want to take the time to do it. I wanted to finish the book.

"What's complicated about ion exchange?" He was persistent.

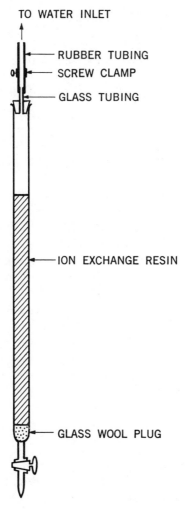

Fig. 19.   Ion exchange column made from a laboratory buret

"Well, for one thing, when dry ion exchange resins are slurred in water, they swell so you have to soak them in water before you put them in a glass column, because otherwise they might swell in the column and break the glass."

"That does not sound very complicated," said Ralph, rubbing his chin.

"Once in a column, the resin should always be kept wet," I went on.

"What's complicated about that?"

I was beginning to become irritated. "And if there are air pockets in the column, the liquid in the column will . . ."

"What will that do?"

"Now look, Ralph, that is what I am trying to explain. The liquid flow through the column will be irregular and this will interfere with adsorption.

"And, Ralph, to prepare a column for use, you have to use distilled water, or at least ion free water, or you will contaminate the column."

"That's no problem," said Ralph. "We have lots of distilled water. But," he added, "how do you get the resin in a column without forming air pockets?"

"You put some water in the buret first and then add the ion exchanger in the form of a slurry."

"And watch it run over the top and onto the desk," he said with a grin.

"You dummy. You have to drain off the extra water but never let the column go dry."

We laughed.

"And you only fill a column about half full of resin."

Ralph grinned, as though this bit of knowledge really made him an expert on ion exchange.

"Before you start, you back wash the column."

"What is that for?" he asked.

"I don't know." I read in the book and then told him. "In order to remove any entrapped air, to classify the resin particles, and to get rid of very fine resin, a water line is attached to the bottom of the column and deionized water is passed upflow through the column. The rate of back wash is increased until the bed expands to fill the whole tube. Then the flow of water is stopped and the bed is allowed to settle by gravity."

"But," said Ralph, "you still haven't told me what is so complicated about it."

"Well, if you must know, the flow of the liquid in ion exchange, the concentration of the solution to be treated, the regeneration process to restore the resin, the time for diffusion of ions into the resin and released ions to diffuse out—all these must be worked out in relation to one another if you are going to develop an effective ion exchange process."

I could tell by the look on his face that this last lecture had snowed him. "But let me tell you something else— ionic species which differ only slightly in their selectivity for ion exchange may be separated in ion exchange chromatography if the column is long enough. Differences in selectivity arise because of ionic size, because of differences of ionization of the ionic species, or differences of the charge on the ions. Once a chromatographic band has been formed in an ion exchange column with two or more ionic species, these can then be further separated by selective elution in which the several adsorbed species are moved through the column at different rates and eventually selectively stripped from the column."

"Oh," said Ralph and he walked out of my lab.

I sat there with a half grin, pleased that Ralph was gone and that I could go back to reading, but the more I thought about it the more guilt I felt for being somewhat abrupt. I got up and followed him into the store room.

"Look Ralph," I said, "this ion exchange. I want to use it to separate rhenium and molybdenum. You know the problem the other fellows were working on." I told him my plans and how I hoped it would work.

He smiled. "Does the professor know what you are up to?"

"No, not yet, but he told me I could work on anything I wanted to and Professor Matthews gave me the resin."

"Don't you think you should tell the professor what you plan to do?"

"I guess so."

Ralph smiled and I figured he knew my thoughts. Our conversation degenerated into small talk and I finally went back to my lab.

I had just finished reading about the different kinds of ion exchange resins when I heard someone walking down the hall. From the shadows through the opaque glass on the upper half of the walls surrounding my laboratory, I knew it was Mary. I looked at my watch. It was a little past noon. I could hardly believe that the morning had gone by so rapidly.

"Well," she said, tossing her head.

"Hi."

"Hello." She smiled. "Are you ready to go?"

I looked at the booklet on my desk, wiggled in my chair, and wondered if I would ever get to the point of understanding enough about ion exchange resins and chromatography so that I could get started on my research. There was a title on the open page, "Strongly Acidic Cation Exchangers." I must have been staring at it, half hypnotized because Mary repeated her question, "Are you ready to go?"

Her voice startled me and I jumped. Somehow I had forgotten that she was there. "Oh."

"Oh?" She tossed her head again. "What does that mean?"

She did not say it, but I could see it written on her face: Why are you ignoring me? I had not meant to ignore her; it was just that my mind was so full of ion exchange and research and chromatography and how I could put it all together for a thesis that I could not turn it off, all at once. But now the daydream was broken and I was back in the real world.

I closed the book. "Let's go," I said.

Outside the sun was shining, and the sky was full of fluffy white clouds. It was like the sky I remembered as a boy in western Canada. There was a huge cloud-horse and a knight with a sword.

Mary broke into my reverie. "What's a strongly acidic cation exchanger?"

"Huh?" I looked at her with a blank look. Once again I realized that my mind had drifted out of the real world and that I had irritated her again.

She said something just as a car started up with a roar. I didn't hear what she said, but I did understand the tone. It was as if she were saying, "You sure aren't any fun today!"

We walked on in silence. I started to feel warm and the palms of my hands got sticky.

"Well, are you going to tell me?" she demanded.

I did not know what to say. "Tell you what?"

"Oh, nothing."

"Look, Mary, I'm really sorry, but . . ."

"You're always sorry." She tossed her head.

"You know, I guess I was born sorry."

We laughed and the tension was broken. "Now tell me, once again, please." I paused for a long time hoping the "please" would penetrate. "What am I supposed to tell you?"

"What is a strongly acidic cation exchanger?"

I was trying to figure out how to explain it to her and I guess there must have been a long period of silence. Anyway she finally added, "Well? Are you going to answer me?"

"Yes, if I can figure out how." I cleared my throat. "Well, strongly acidic cation exchangers contain sulfonic acid groups anchored to a resin."

"What are sulfonic acid groups?"

Just then a squirrel ran out on a limb of a tree almost directly in front of us. A second squirrel was chasing the first.

"Looks like fun," I said. "Remember when you used to chase me."

She looked at me and smiled and for a moment I thought she had forgotten her question, but it was not long until she said, "Well?"

"Sulfonic acid groups." I ran my fingers through my hair and pushed up the nosepiece of my glasses. "Do you remember what sulfuric acid is?"

Every time we had to dilute H_2SO_4 in the laboratory I used to recite a little verse. She looked at me in disgust and said, "Put the water in before you add the H_2SO_4." She chuckled as if to remind me how many times she had heard me say it.

"Well, a strongly acidic cation exchanger is like sulfuric acid. That is, its reactions are like those of sulfuric acid except that the active groups are really not in solution but attached to a resin. The resin has the ability to pull ions out of solution."

"What are active groups?"

"You know what? If I was born sorry, you were born asking questions." I looked at her and smiled, and she smiled too. "And I guess you will die asking questions."

"I want to know," she said.

"But why?"

"I don't know. I just want to know."

Again I ran my fingers through my hair. I had not really had that much time to study the whole thing myself, and how do you explain something before it is organized in your mind?

"Are you going to tell me?"

"The active groups are sulfonic acid groups." The minute I said it I realized that she had asked me what a sulfonic acid group was and I had not really told her. "If sulfuric acid reacts with an organic molecule, part of the sulfuric acid can be tied to an organic tail. The part of the sulfuric acid that sticks on the organic is called a sulfonic acid group. So the hybrid molecule is really half like sulfuric acid and half like the organic tail."

"Is it really a hybrid molecule?"

"I don't know. I just made that part up."

"How am I supposed to know if you just make it up as you talk?"

We laughed. "Anyway," I said, "when a sulfonic acid group is attached to a resin, a big hunk of organic, these groups try to act like sulfuric acid, but since the group is anchored to the resin, it can't really act like it."

"It does and it doesn't. Now isn't that clear!"

"Not really. Sulfuric acid ionizes in water. So sulfonic acid groups on a resin attract different ions—cations— like hydrogen ions or sodium ions or calcium ions. Such resins in contact with solutions which contain several kinds of cations trade one ion for another, but each sulfonic acid group has only one negative charge available so it can attract only one cation. That's why they are called cation exchangers. The strongly acidic part is because sulfuric acid is a strong acid, or highly ionized, and the sulfonic acid group on the resin acts the same way."

We had reached the front porch of the house where we had the upstairs apartment. "What do you want for lunch?" she asked me.

"You mean I've got a choice?"

She smiled. "That's what I said."

"How about French toast?"

I sat down at the kitchen table and picked up a book as Mary went to the refrigerator to get the eggs. I had hoped that my interest in the book would end the cross-examination, but it didn't.

"What good are strongly acidic cation exchange resins?" she continued.

I looked up from the book. "I don't know."

"What are they used for?"

"You just asked me that, and I said I didn't know."

"That's what you always say when you don't want to talk."

"Do you really want to know or do you just want to talk?"

She shrugged. "I guess I want to know."

"Well, when a hydrogen ion neutralizes the charge on the sulfonic acid group, cation exchange resins in the hydrogen form can be used to neutralize a basic solution. The resin trades a hydrogen ion for the cation of the base, and the released hydrogen ion reacts with the hydroxide ion of the base to form water. Come here and I'll show you the reaction of a resin and sodium hydroxide."

I wrote the reaction on a piece of paper:

$$RSO_3H + Na^+ + OH^- \longrightarrow RSO_3Na + H_2O$$

"So instead of dumping alkaline solutions—wastes—in sewers to pollute the rivers and lakes, you can adsorb the alkali with a strongly acidic cation exchanger," I said.

"Oh."

"You can also use these resins in combination with an anion exchange resin to completely deionize water. Strongly acidic cation exchangers can split salts."

"Split a salt. What does that mean?"

"Take a salt, like sodium chloride." I paused. "In the hydrogen form, the resin can exchange its hydrogen ions for sodium ions of the salt, leaving hydrochloric acid. Do you want to see the reaction?"

Even before she could answer, I had written that equation below the first:

$$RSO_3H + Na^+ + Cl^- \rightleftarrows RSO_3Na + H^+ + Cl^-$$

"Now, if you have an anion exchanger which can exchange chloride ions for hydroxide, then you can take all the cations out with the sulfonic acid resin and all the anions out, and you have deionized water. Many places are now using deionized water instead of distilled water because deionized water costs less."

"Oh." She paused and then added, "Are you ready to eat?"

I thought that lunch would bring an end to talk about ion exchange resins, but the interrogation continued.

Between mouthfuls Mary asked, "Why don't they just call them cation exchange resins?"

"They do."

"Well, then, what is this strongly acidic?"

When Mary was in a questioning mood, the questions never stopped. I was about to ask if she really wanted to know but instead I took a deep breath and started the explanation. "There is a kind of cation ion exchange resin in which the active groups are —COOH. The reactions of this group are analogous to those of acetic acid. Acetic acid is a weak acid; that is, it tends to hold on to hydrogen ions. In other words, acetic acid is only slightly ionized. This type of ion exchange resin, sometimes called a carboxylic type cation exchanger, is not reactive toward neutral salts, and it is only slightly active in weakly acidic solutions. Because of the strong tendency to hold hydrogen ions, these resins are easily regenerated with acids."

She looked at me and smiled. I wasn't sure if she really understood what I had just said. For that matter, I wasn't sure I did either. "How did you like the ion exchange lunch?" I asked her.

"If we don't hurry," she replied, "I'm going to be late for work."

We were just leaving the front porch when she asked, "Which of these resins are you going to use . . . to do . . . well, whatever it is you are going to do?"

"Neither."

"Well why are you spending all your time reading about that stuff then? How come we've been talking all noon about these whatever-they-are?"

I took a deep breath and counted to 10. "Just because you've been asking me all sorts of questions."

We walked on in silence. The silence finally got the best of me and I asked her if she wanted to get together with the Hansens again on Sunday (Gaurth Hansen was a graduate student in biochemistry).

She said she did, and in the same sentence asked me another question, "Why are you reading about ion exchange resins then?"

"Well," I started slowly. "I want to separate rhenium from molybdenum, perrhenic acid from molybdic acid, that is. Perrhenate and molybdate are anions, negatively charged, so they will be or should be adsorbed on anion exchange resins. These are like cation exchange resins except that their active groups carry a positive charge, and therefore they attract and exchange negative ions." I paused and looked at her to try to tell if she was really listening.

"Go on."

"Just like cation exchangers there are two kinds of anion exchangers—strongly basic and weakly basic. The strongly basic ones have a strongly basic group attached to the resin and the weakly basic . . . well you get the point, don't you?"

She nodded.

Then I added, "The strongly basic exchangers act like sodium hydroxide and the weakly basic like the weakly alkaline ammonium hydroxide. Amberlite IR–4B, the resin that Professor Matthews gave me, is a weakly basic anion exchange resin."

"Is that the one you're going to use to separate rhenium and that other thing?"

"Yes."

"Why?"

"Because that's the resin I've got."

"That's not a good reason."

Mary was right. But it annoyed me to have her say it. I was all mixed up inside. Besides being annoyed at her question, I was frustrated because I didn't know the answer and because I wasn't really sure that the ion exchange thing would work out anyway. I was thankful that Mary wasn't going to be my thesis examination committee.

"Well, perrhenate ion has a single charge and molybdate has two. Molybdic acid is not as strong an acid, I think."

"Don't you know?"

I ignored her question. "Molybdate sometimes forms polyions and . . ." I paused. I was about to say I didn't think perrhenate did, but I changed my mind. "Anyway I am convinced that there are enough differences between these two anions to allow me to separate them with an anion exchange resin."

"Are you going to use a strong or weak resin?"

A car screeched to a halt at the stoplight, leaving a long patch of black on the road. I looked at her and raised my eyebrows.

"Well?"

"You mean strongly basic or weakly basic don't you?"

"I guess so."

"Well, Amberlite IR–4B is weakly basic. The active groups on this resin are amines." I paused. Again I was about to say "I think," but I didn't. "It seems to me with a weakly basic resin I have two chances for success: the difference in charge on perrhenate and molybdate and the possibility that one is a weaker acid than the other."

She looked at me, and I sensed that her next question was really going to put me on the spot. "Well," she began, "which of these, perrhenate or the other one, is going to be more strongly adsorbed?"

"I wish I knew. I guess that depends on a number of things like the acidity of the solution. Actually they would both be adsorbed, but I hope to different degrees."

"If that happens how do you ever hope to get them separated?"

"By adsorbing them both in a column and then washing one out."

"With what?"

"I don't know. I guess if it were that simple, everyone would know the answer and I wouldn't have the basis for a thesis—at least not a Ph.D. thesis. I guess that's what I have to figure out."

When I got back to my laboratory, I looked through the booklet on ion exchange to see if what I had told her about ion exchange resins was correct. I made a table in my notebook, just so I would have it neatly organized for myself, on the analogies of ion exchange resins and acids and bases:

Acid or Base	Type	Ion Exchanger	Formula
Sulfuric acid	strong acid	sulfonic acid	RSO_3H
Acetic acid	weak acid	carboxylic acid	$ROOOH$
Sodium hydroxide	strong base	quarternary ammonium	$RN(CH_3)_3OH$

Acid or Base	*Type*	*Ion Exchanger*	*Formula*
Ammonium hydroxide	weak base	amine	RNH_2

Then I reviewed the reactions of weakly basic anion exchange resins, like Amberlite IR–4B, to try to convince myself that my idea was a good one:

$$RNH_2 + H^+ + Cl^- \longrightarrow RNH_3Cl$$

$$RNH_3Cl + ReO_4^- \rightleftarrows RNH_3ReO_4 + Cl^-$$

After I was all finished, I sat there wondering: can I really find a way to separate perrhenate and molybdate with Amberlite IR–4B? Which one will be more strongly adsorbed? If I put them both on a column, what can I use to wash one of them out?

CHAPTER 6

The Plan

I expected that the perrhenate ion would be more strongly adsorbed than molybdate ion by Amberlite IR–4B, even though molybdate was dibasic. There were several reasons for my hunch. Perrhenate is more acidic. Moreover, molybdate forms polyanions in solution. Typical of these is dimolybdate:

$$MoO_4{}^{2-} + 2H^+ \rightleftharpoons Mo_2O_7{}^{2-} + H_2O$$

Polyanions like $Mo_2O_7{}^{2-}$ are larger and hence might be more difficult to fit into the crowded pores of an anion exchange resin. It's like trying to fit a man's foot into a child's shoe.

When a scientist has an idea, he likes to talk it over with someone for several reasons. One reason is to reorganize his thinking; ideas usually come in a crude state and need considerable revision and refinement. Another reason is that a scientist is usually proud of his ideas. Like a baseball player who has just hit a home run, he likes to have the recognition and admiration of his colleagues. The more I thought about my idea of trying to separate perrhenic and molybdic acids chromatographically, the more I felt this way. I wanted to discuss the idea with some other chemist.

But I didn't. At the time I was the only graduate student working for Professor Meloche. As a matter of fact, immediately following the war there were hardly any graduate students in the chemistry department at

Wisconsin. There was hardly anyone with whom to discuss my idea except the professors on the staff.

I was determined to discuss my idea with Professor Meloche but only after I had worked it out in the laboratory. As I think back about it now, I can't justify my stubbornness. Actually I am somewhat disconcerted by the fact that I didn't discuss my research program with my major professor. It's certainly not the kind of thing that's common. But, I was young and axious and prejudiced. I was anxious to get started and to see if the idea would work. Besides that, it had been five years since I started graduate school—two of which had been spent on the Manhattan project—so I was anxious to get finished. And like many young graduate students I was cocky; I had the feeling that if left alone, I could complete my research just as fast as if I had help.

Besides, as far as I knew, Professor Meloche had never had any experience in chromatographic techniques; none of his former students had worked in the field, and I assumed that he knew no more than I about the subject.

When I talked it over with Mary that evening, she was not nearly as confident as I. "What if you spend six months or a year on your idea," she said, "only to find that you are not successful?"

I stared out the window of our second floor apartment. It was autumn and the leaves had already started to fall. "Boy," I said. "You've got a lot of confidence in me."

She blushed. "It's not that, really. I guess you can do it." She turned around and looked straight at me. "You're the one who's been telling me that a Ph.D. is like having the right name, or being born on the right side of the tracks."

"So?"

"So why do you want to make the professor angry by going off on your own?"

"Look." I paused, but only for a moment. "I've no intention of making Professor Meloche angry. I don't think he really cares what I do for my thesis. I think letting me go off on my own is one of the ways the professor has of teaching me something. I think he wants me to be independent."

"That's what you think he thinks. But is that really what he thinks?"

Even if she had a point, I couldn't admit it. Maybe it was pride. Maybe it was a need to develop self-assurance. I'm still not sure, but I'd made a decision, and I was determined to see it through—even if it meant spending an extra year in graduate school. At that time, the possibility of failure seemed very remote.

The more I thought about it, the more definite I became. It's a lot more fun, I thought, to work on your own ideas. Somehow there's just more satisfaction in doing something all the way by yourself.

And yet, I wasn't at graduate school alone. Mary was as anxious to get through school as I was. She wanted the finer things in life. She'd never complained, and yet I knew that she longed for the time when we would have a home of our own instead of living out of a suitcase in an apartment.

The more I thought about her feelings, the more confused I became. There was really no way to know which was the better way. And then I had that one sickening thought: what if I should be successful in chromatographically separating perrhenic and molybdic acids only to find that the university would not approve this for a Ph.D. thesis?

As I sat in my laboratory one afternoon and thought of these things, I decided that indecision could be as disastrous as the wrong decision. I made up my mind. I would take the risk and go it alone.

Having made the decision once and for all, I resolved that I must formulate a thorough and careful plan for my research. Like the perfect crime, I wanted no chance for failure. As a result, I spent the next several days in the library reading, planning, thinking, and reorganizing. I read and reread chapters from a book on adsorption until the Freundlich isotherm became so fixed in my mind that I would see it in my dreams.

I read statements like, "It is difficult to predict, without experiment, whether an adsorbent will be active under a given set of conditions." What if for some crazy reason, Amberlite ion exchange resin would not adsorb perrhenate ions?

In one of the books I found a list of the conditions which generally increase or decrease adsorption, and I read the list several times, trying to decide which factors I could use in my study:

"1. The surface area of an adsorbent is an important factor in determining the amount of substance which can be adsorbed per gram of adsorbent." There was no way that I could change the surface area of Amberlite IR–4B, but from my reading about it I assumed it was porous like a sponge and that, in effect, it had a very large surface area.

"2. Adsorption efficiency increases as concentration decreases." This means that adsorption studies should be conducted from dilute solutions.

"3. An adsorbent tends to adsorb a given solute most strongly from solvents in which it (the solute) is the least soluble." I wondered if I could apply this principle to my problem.

"4. Adsorption reactions are not as rapid as ionic ones; however, equilibrium is usually complete in a manner of minutes." Desorption is a relatively slow process. This means that in my studies of chromatographic separation of rhenium and molybdenum I might be able to use one effect against the other.

"5. Increasing the temperature usually favors decreasing adsorption." With an ion exchange resin I assumed I would work at room temperature, so I gave this factor no further thought.

"6. Many solids can be activated, and after being activated they are stronger adsorbents." This was really not a concern either, as far as ion exchange resins were concerned. They were tailor made to do a specific job, and if they were going to work, they would work. If not, well . . .

"7. In some cases adsorption is so strong that an adsorbent can be used but once." Other adsorbents may be regenerated and used in a cyclic process. I knew that ion exchange resins could be regenerated.

"8. The adsorbing power of different solids varies enormously.

"9. Adsorption is preferential in many cases, *i.e.*, the specific adsorbent may adsorb one solute more strongly and in greater quantity than the second solute. Predictions as to which species might be preferentially adsorbed are difficult to make unless the mechanism of adsorption is understood—as when a chemical reaction is involved." As I read this, I wondered whether it would be possible to change the nature of the perrhenate or molybdate ion by, for example, adding something that would complex with either or both of these and thus change the extent to which they would be ion exchanged. For instance, I knew that molybdate tends to form polymeric anions; I knew that it formed complexes with many organic compounds.

One afternoon I found a new book on chromatography. From it I read, once again, the account of Tswett's early experiments, and reviewed in my mind the meaning of such terms as chromatogram, development, elution, and breakthrough. When a solvent containing a single solute is passed through a chromatographic column, a uniform band will be formed in the column. If adsorption–desorption equilibrium is maintained, this band should maintain sharp edges and constant width on development provided the same solvent is used in development as was used in formation. When a different solvent is used, the width of the band will change to a new value, and on reaching this value it will remain constant in width with sharp edges on further development. The rate of development can be calculated in either case if the adsorption isotherm for the solvent is known.

In actual practice, rate and equilibrium both play a role. Hence diffuse boundaries are usually formed in a chromatographic column, and calculations based on equilibrium alone are usually inaccurate.

But the statement which really gave me hope was one which said that by pouring a solvent through a chromatographic column, the bands of different solutes are washed through the column at different rates, and if a sufficiently long column and a sufficiently large volume of developing agent are used, it is theoretically possible to effect the complete separation of a chromatogram into the discrete bands of each adsorbed material separated by bands of adsorbent only.

I decided to make a list of the factors which affected the behavior and operating capacity of anion exchange resins, hoping that this would give clues as to the best way to attack the problem. My list consisted of eight factors:

1. The nature of the resin itself. This factor includes not only the chemical components which were used to prepare the resin but the freedom of the active sites after polymerization. For example, ion exchangers in which the amino groups have been tied up by polymerization, formation of the resin, show capacity below theoretical. It's as if the active sites were handcuffed.

2. The strength of the acid to be adsorbed. Strong acids are readily and completely adsorbed while weak ones may be only partially adsorbed or not adsorbed at all, depending on their ionization constants.

3. The basicity of the acid to be adsorbed. The ion exchange capacity for a divalent acid like sulfuric is greater than for a monobasic acid like hydrochloric.

4. The influent concentration. Lower concentrations favor more efficient adsorption.

5. The molecular size of the acid to be adsorbed. Steric (size and shape) factors are known to have an appreciable effect on the adsorption of ions by resinous ion exchangers (the man's foot in the boy's shoe).

6. The operating conditions. This includes the rate of percolation through the column (do ions move too rapidly to be caught?) and size and shape of the bed. The longer the bed (the more poker chips in the stack), the better.

7. The pH of the influent solution. As the pH of the solution increases, the tendency for adsorption decreases. This factor is important in elution, in the release of adsorbed ions. The adsorption of anion from solution of its salts may vary with the cation of the salt. Thus adsorption of sulfate from ammonium sulfate would be considerably more than from sodium sulfate. The reason is that ammonium sulfate hydrolyzes to give a solution of lower pH than the unhydrolyzed sodium sulfate.

$$2NH_4^+ + SO_4^{2-} + 2H_2O \longrightarrow 2NH_4OH + 2H^+ + SO_4^{2-}$$

8. The history of the resin prior to its use. Resins which are fully swollen have a higher capacity than dried resins. When practical, ion exchange resins should be soaked for several hours before use.

That evening after dinner I was sitting on the edge of our bed going over the list. Mary was in the other room listening to the radio. Finally she came in and sat down beside me.

"Well," she said, "what did you do today?"

I showed her the list. "Read mostly," I said, "and thought. I'm still convinced it will work, but nowhere have I found any clue as to the best conditions for adsorbing perrhenate and the worst conditions for molybdate."

"Why don't you do it the other way?"

"I guess it doesn't really matter," I said. "Somehow I've gotten used to thinking about adsorbing perrhenate while leaving molybdate in solution. I guess that's because flue dust concentrate has so much molybdenum and so little rhenium, and it's the rhenium that we've been trying to extract."

She smiled at me. "You're always trying to figure out an easier way to save work. Why don't you just do it?"

"That's just the problem. I don't really know where to begin."

"It seems simple enough to me. All you do is put some of that stuff in a buret and pour the solution through it. Isn't that what you said?"

"Maybe that's what I said once, but now I'm convinced it's not that simple. When I pour a solution of perrhenate and molybdate through a column of Amberlite IR–4B, both ions will be adsorbed to some extent, even if one is more strongly adsorbed. I've got to find a way to wash the weakly adsorbed one out without losing the other one. The question is: what's the best way preferentially to elute the molybdate?"

"Well," she said as if it were still very simple, "how are you going to find out?"

"That's just what I've been wondering. Batch experiments might be the quickest way to get the clues."

Mary brushed her hair back. "What do you mean by that?"

"Well," I started slowly. "If I stir some resin with molybdate in one case and perrhenate in another, both at the same pH and everything, I can measure the equilibrium adsorption of each. All I have to do is find a set of conditions that favor perrhenate adsorption and not molybdate adsorption, and those are the conditions to use to develop the chromatogram."

"To do what?"

"To elute preferentially or remove the molybdate while leaving the perrhenate."

"You mean you're going to do batch experiments and then run a column. Why don't you find the best conditions in a column to start with?"

It now seemed clear to me, even if I couldn't explain it to her. "Because," I said, "I can run 25 batch experiments for each column experiment. If I start with a column and I'm lucky on the first try, that would be great. But if I'm not, I've got to start over. In the meantime, if I run several batch studies I'll know which are the best column conditions for success before I ever set up a column."

CHAPTER 7

Batch Experiments

It was raining the morning that I ran the series of batch experiments, but I was anxious to get started and paid no attention to the weather. To be sure that the experiments would be comparable, one to another, I prepared a large batch of resin by regenerating with a 5% solution of sodium carbonate, washing with distilled water, and air-drying. The air-dried resin had a weight loss at 110°C of 41%. Next, I wrote up an experimental procedure:

• In each experiment use 2 grams of resin in 100 ml of solution.

• Run experiments in duplicate.

• In experiments with rhenium, use 5 ml of a stock solution of $KReO_4$ containing 50 μgrams of rhenium per milliliter, and in the experiments with molybdenum, 10 ml of a stock solution of ammonium molybdate containing 100 μgrams of molybdenum per milliliter.

• Add other acid solutions and then dilute to 100 ml, add the resin, and stir in a 125-ml Erlenmeyer flask for 10 minutes.

• Filter and analyze the filtrate for the rhenium or molybdenum and any other reagents, and for pH.

In my first set of experiments, I added different amounts of sulfuric acid with a fixed amount of perrhenic acid and then did a duplicate series with a fixed amount of molybdic acid. I allowed for the substantial time that would be involved in set-up for these experiments, but it took longer than I had expected to gather stirrers, make stock solutions, set up the apparatus, do the experiments, run the analyses, and measure pH. By the time I finished taking the last reading on the colorimeter it was just past five, time to meet Mary. I wanted to make the calculations, but I knew she'd be waiting.

"What's your problem?" she asked as she saw me coming around the corner in the hall of the chemistry building.

"Nothing, really, it's just that I didn't have time to make the calculations. Why don't you go home and fix dinner, and I'll come in a little bit?"

She smiled. "I know your 'little bits.' You'll get interested and forget to come home. Why don't I go pick up a couple of hamburgers and malts and bring them up to your lab?"

"You're kidding," I said, but from the way she smiled I knew she wasn't.

I went back to the laboratory, and by the time she got back with the hamburgers, I'd finished the calculations (Table 3).

Table 3. Adsorption of Perrhenic, Molybdic, and Sulfuric Acids by Two Grams of Amberlite IR–4B

H_2SO_4 Original, N	% $HReO_4$ Adsorbed	% H_2MoO_4 Adsorbed	% H_2SO_4 Adsorbed	Final pH
0.0114	94	89	87	2.77
0.0570	71	64	64	1.68
0.114	57	52	48	1.28
0.570	24	19	21	0.50
1.08	16	10	17	0.22

"Well . . . finished?" she asked as she came through the door.

"Yeah."

"You don't sound very happy."

"I'm not. There's hardly any difference at all."

"Let me see."

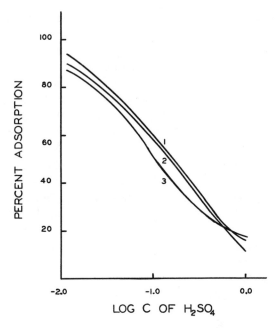

Fig. 20. The adsorption of perrhenate (1), molybdate (2), and sulfate (3) by Amberlite IR-4B from solutions containing 250 micrograms of rhenium as perrhenate, 1000 micrograms of molybdenum as molybdate, and varying amounts of sulfuric acid.

I showed her the data. She didn't seem to be the least bit discouraged. "Why don't you plot them? They might look different on graph paper. How do you calculate the exchange constants, or whatever you call them? What are you going to try next?"

I sat back in my chair. "Those hamburgers smell good. Let's eat."

We ate, but my mind never left the experiment. "I wonder," I said as we were finishing, "if phosphoric acid would be better. It complexes with molybdic acid, and maybe the size of the complex . . ."

"Why don't you try it?" she cut in. "You show me what to do and I'll do it while you draw the graphs."

Mary had taken some college chemistry, and during the day she worked in a laboratory at the university, so it didn't take long for me to explain to her what to do.

The first graph that I drew was a plot of the percent adsorption *vs.* the log of the normality of the H_2SO_4 (Figure 20). As I had suspected from looking at the data, the curves were bunched; there was no strong tendency for adsorption of any of the three and, while a separation under such conditions might be possible, my instinct told me that it would take an extremely long column.

I looked at the data and wondered whether the adsorption by ion-exchange resins followed the Freundlich isotherm, and I decided to calculate the milliequivalents of sulfuric acid adsorbed per gram of resin and the concentration of sulfuric acid after adsorption. They are plotted in Figure 21.

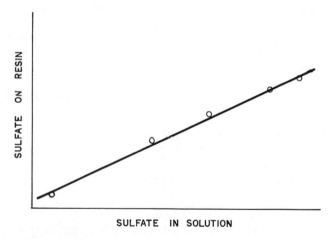

Fig. 21. The adsorption isotherm for sulfate on Amberlite IR-4B (a log–log plot).

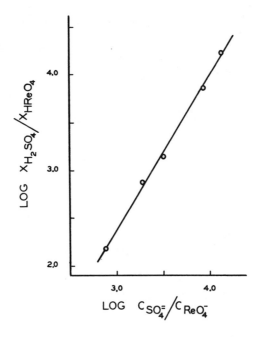

Fig. 22. Sulfate–perrhenate anion exchange—on Amberlite IR-4B.

It looked just like graphs that I'd seen in the textbooks. I don't know why I was so surprised. I guess it was that for the first time in my life I had applied a theory that I had learned from books, and it worked out just as predicted. Somehow, I had expected that research would be more difficult.

After I finished plotting the figure, I sat there looking at it and thinking about anion exchange. I made some calculation, shown in the Appendix, from which I deduced an equation for anion exchange. From the data in Table III for use in the equation, I calculated the sulfate/perrhenate ratios in solution and on the resin, and from these ratios I plotted the exchange reaction in Figure

22. I did the same thing for sulfate/molybdate to get Figure 23.

"Look," I said as I showed the graphs to Mary, "they're straight lines."

"What does that mean?"

I scratched my head. "I don't know." I looked at the graphs again. "Anyway, they look nice."

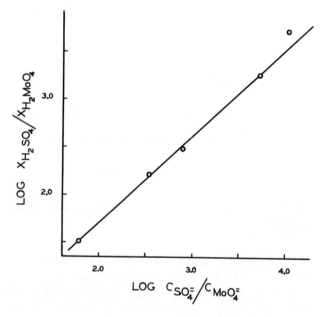

Fig. 23. Sulfate–molybdate anion exchange—on Amberlite IR-4B.

She smiled at me. "Does it tell you how to separate perrhenate and molybdate?"

"Not really." I sat there thinking about her question. From the way I had drawn the graphs there really was no way to compare the relative adsorption of molybdate and perrhenate. As a matter of fact, the more I looked at the graphs, the more sure I became that they had no meaning with regard to my problem at all.

"Well," I said, "what a waste."

But I couldn't stop staring at the graphs and the equations. If I rearranged equation 7.2 another way I could compare the ratios of A on the resin and in solution with that of B on the resin and in solution. Thus I could compare sulfate with molybdate in one case and with perrhenate in the other. And I could use sulfate as a reference to compare the relative adsorbability of perrhenate with molybdate. I looked back at Figure 20 and got the feeling that this would be an exercise in futility, but I decided to do it anyway.

I rearranged equation 7.2 as follows:

$$K = \frac{(X_A/C_{A-})}{(X_B/C_{B-})} \qquad (7.4)$$

I then wrote equation 7.4 in logarithmic form:

$$\log (X_A/C_A^-) = \log K + \log (X_B/C_B^-)$$

For simplicity, I rewrote the equation:

$$\log (X/C)_A = \log K + \log (X/C)_B \qquad (7.5)$$

Letting A represent sulfate in each case and B represent perrhenate or molybdate, whichever the case might be, I could now make a graph which would allow me to compare directly the relative adsorbability of the two anions that I was trying to separate. I plotted Figure 24 and showed the new graph to Mary.

"Look," I said, "the exchange reactions for sulfate–perrhenate and for sulfate–molybdate are straight lines, and they are parallel."

"What's so great about that?"

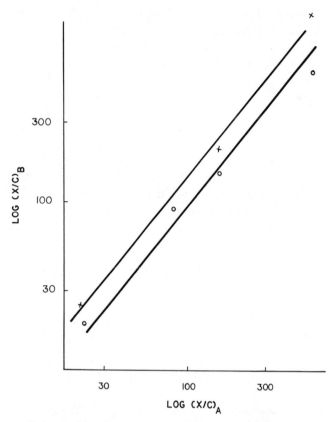

Fig. 24. Comparison of the relative adsorbability of perrhenate and molybdate vs. sulfate from solutions of pH below 3 on Amberlite IR-4B.

"Nothing, I guess. Anyway, the lines are rather close together and I suspect that under the conditions the experimental error could account for the difference. I mean I guess that there is really no big difference in the tendency for the resin to adsorb molybdate or perrhenate." I looked up at her. "How is the experiment with phosphoric acid coming?"

"I'm nearly finished," she said. "All we have to do is analyze these filtrates."

She had 10 Erlenmeyer flasks lined up neatly on the lab bench, each one labelled. Five contained perrhenic–phosphoric, and five contained molybdic–phosphoric acids.

"If you'll take pH and titrate each solution for acidity, I'll run the rhenium and moly analysis," I said.

It was after 11 when we finished, and she really looked tired. I had a feeling that we should go home, but I knew I wouldn't sleep if I didn't know what the results were. "Tell you what," I said, "I'll take the notebook home and make the calculations there, and in the meantime you can go to bed."

I went in the kitchen to work on the table there, so I wouldn't disturb her. When I was finished, I made a table of the data, Table 4.

Table 4. Adsorption of Perrhenic, Molybdic, and Phosphoric Acids by Two Grams of Amberlite IR–4B

H_3PO_4 Original, N	% $HReO_4$ Adsorbed	% H_2MoO_4 Adsorbed	% H_3PO_4 Adsorbed	Final pH
0.0118	100	88	93	3.68
0.0589	98	88	89	2.59
0.118	95	96	77	2.11
0.589	80	93	52	1.39
1.12	68	84	45	1.15

I looked at the data—I couldn't believe it. The behavior of molybdic acid was completely unreasonable . . . unless . . . unless there were a phosphomolybdate complex formed which had a strong influence on the extent to which molybdic acid was picked up by the resin.

One thing was sure; phosphoric acid didn't impress me as a medium for the chromatographic separation of perrhenic and molybdic acids. I went to bed, discouraged.

The next morning I plotted the data (Figures 25 and 26).

The behavior of perrhenic–phosphoric acids was as I had expected, but the molybdic–phosphoric plot didn't seem to obey any kind of rules. I was torn between trying to figure out what was happening and finding a way of separating perrhenate and molybdate chromatographically.

I suspected that the reason for the unexpected behavior was the formation of phosopho–molybdic acid complexes. I decided the formation of the complex increased the tendency for molybdic acid to be adsorbed. I wondered if there were complexes which would decrease that tendency.

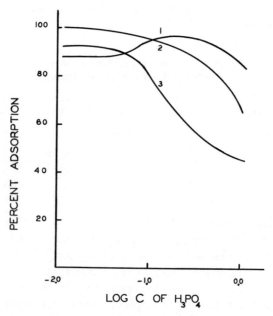

Fig. 25. The adsorption of molybdate (1), perrhenate (2), and phosphate (3) by Amberlite IR-4B.

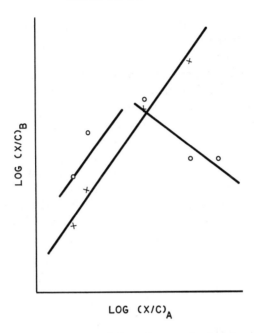

Fig. 26. Comparison of the relative adsorbability of perrhenate and molybdate vs. phosphate on Amberlite IR-4B.

I met Mary at noon, and we went to the student cafeteria for lunch. At first we just talked, but finally she asked if I'd figured out why the experiment we'd run the night before had come out as it did.

"It's because phosphoric acid and molybdic acid form complexes," I said, "and these are more strongly adsorbed than molybdic acid alone."

"Oh."

"I've been thinking," I continued, "I wonder how the complex would behave with boric acid?"

In science a single idea often leads to unexpected discoveries, and this is what happened to me. I must confess that it took me a lot longer to recognize what was happening than now seems reasonable. But that's often the case. Once you understand something it can seem obvious and simple, but until you do it, it seems difficult and complex.

In the first experiment that I ran with boric acid addition, I found a slight decrease in the amount of adsorption of molybdic acid as the amount of boric acid was increased. However, I ran a second series at a lower acidity and found the reverse effect (Figure 27)! In an attempt to get at the reason I finally decided to investigate the effect of 0.2M boric acid on the sulfate–molybdate exchange. When I plotted the data (Figure 28), I noted a decided break in the plot. Why? At first I thought it had to do with a complex between boric acid and molybdic acid, but the more I thought about it, the more

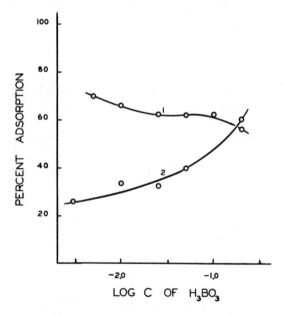

Fig. 27. The adsorption of molybdate on Amberlite IR-4B from sulfuric acid–boric acid solutions: (1) 0.0114N sulfuric acid; (2) 0.0000285N sulfuric acid.

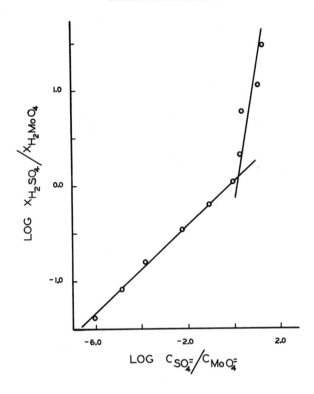

Fig. 28. Sulfate–molybdate anion exchange on Amberlite IR-4B.

unreal this idea seemed. When your mind gets in a rut, it's sometimes hard to consider the alternatives. That's what happened to me until some days later when I was looking at the data—the same data I had looked at 100 times—I first really thought about what I was looking at. As less sulfuric acid was used, the pH got higher. Once I thought about the effect of acidity, I began to wonder how this affected the resin itself. Amberlite IR–4B is not an effective exchange resin in alkaline solutions. Maybe exchange takes place in two steps:

$$RNH_2 + H^+ = RNH_3^+$$
$$RNH_3^+ + A^- = RNH_3A$$

where RNH_2 is the active group of the resin and A^- is the anion which is adsorbed. Adsorption of an anion from solution is a result of the electrostatic attraction between the RNH_3^+ form of the resin and the anion. To preserve the neutrality of the resin and the solution, it follows that the first reaction is always accompanied by

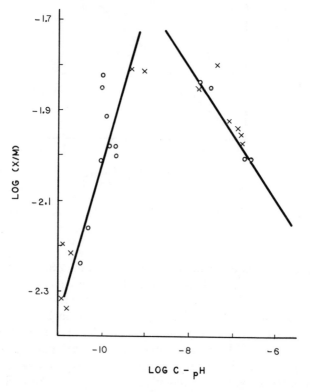

Fig. 29. Isotherm for adsorption of molybdate on Amberlite IR-4B.

the second. It also follows that there will be no adsorption if the resin is in the RNH_2 state.

I decided to write the Freundlich isotherm which represents adsorption in the form:

$$(x/m) = K(a_H^+ \cdot a_A^-)^{1/n} \qquad (7.6)$$

whence:

$$\log (x/m) = \log K + 1/n \log (a_H^+ \cdot a_A^-)$$
$$= \log K - 1/n \, pH + 1/n \log (a_A^-) \qquad (7.7)$$

I decided to use the equation 7.7 to plot all the data of molybdic acid to see what would happen.

There was a lot of scatter in the plot (Figure 29) but one thing surprised me more than anything else; the data with and without boric acid all blended together. Apparently the bend in the plot of Figure 28 is not caused by a boric acid complex.

I explained the scatter, to myself at least, on the fact that some of the resin may have dried out, that in some cases 10 minutes may not have been long enough to reach equilibrium, that the analytical methods I used may have shown variation, and that human error could be involved. But I still had no explanation for the bend in my graphs.

About that time one of the students in second year chemistry asked me to help him balance the equation for the reaction of chromate to dichromate:

$$2CrO_4^{2-} + 2H^+ \longrightarrow Cr_2O_7^{2-} + H_2O$$

It was then that I remembered reading about the polymerization of molybdic acid. The first step in the polymerization is exactly like the reaction for chromate to dichromate:

$$2MoO_4^{2-} + 2H^+ \longrightarrow Mo_2O_7^{2-} + H_2O$$

Could the conversion of molybdate to dimolybdate be the reason for the breaks in Figures 30 and 31? That had to be the reason. I looked again at Figure 31. It all seemed so simple now. Not only that, but I could now understand why pH didn't affect the extent to which perrhenate was adsorbed, at least up to pH 7. Perrhenate doesn't polymerize. I was sure I now had the basis for separating rhenium and molybdenum. I could hardly wait to tell Mary.

"It's all over," I said. "I'm finished with my thesis."

She looked perplexed. "You mean you made a chromatographic separation this afternoon?"

"Well, not exactly. But I figured out how to do it."

"Hurray!"

"Would you like to know how?"

She smiled.

"It's all a matter of pH! At pH 5–7, perrhenic acid is completely adsorbed by Amberlite IR–4B, and molybdic acid only 25 or 30% adsorbed."

I fully expected her to share my excitement, but she didn't. All she said was, "So?"

"So I know how to do it."

"Don't count your chickens before ..."

"Who's counting chickens?" I cut in. "It has to work. I know it. So who's counting chickens?"

She looked right at me. "You."

CHAPTER 8

Interviews

One of the things that made life as a graduate student at Wisconsin exciting was the interviews. A constant stream of men from industry visited the university to talk to the graduate students about future employment. One of the men I talked with was Dr. John Reynard of Du Pont.

At the outset, Dr. Reynard told me about Du Pont and about Wilmington, and finally he asked me about my thesis topic. "I'm really just getting started," I said. "I'm try to separate perrhenic and molybdic acids chromatographically." I told him about my ideas.

"I didn't know that Professor Meloche was interested in chromatography," he said.

"He's not really. I chose the topic myself."

Talk of chromatography made me curious to know whether I might have a chance to use the specific things I'd learned as a graduate student if I accepted a job with Du Pont, so I asked Dr. Reynard, "Are chromatographic techniques used much in industry?"

"Do you mean in Du Pont, specifically?"

"Well . . . yes."

"One of our departments, Industrial and Biochemicals, uses gas chromatography constantly to analyze for residues of herbicides and pesticides in soil and plant tissue."

I pondered that one. "Gas chromatography? Let's see . . . How does that work?"

He paused for a moment. "In principle, it's much like the research you plan to do with ion exchangers, except the moving phase is a gas, not an aqueous solution. The stationary phase can be a solid or a liquid."

"How can you pass a gas through a liquid, and get a chromatographic effect?"

He smiled. "Actually, it's a liquid of low volatility held on an inert, solid support."

"Oh, then I suppose that the difference in solubility of the components of the gas stream is the basis for separation."

We went on to discuss the details of gas chromatography. Differences in solubilities and adsorption allow components to move through the column at different rates. If the column is long enough, the components emerge as distinct peaks or zones separated by essentially pure carrier gas. The problem is to identify the component(s) in the presence of the carrier gas. This is generally done by instrumental methods with an automatic recorder recording the results.

"Have any of the results of Du Pont work on gas chromatography been published?" I asked.

"As a matter of fact, yes." Dr. Reynard paused. "Jack Kirkland publishes frequently. He collaborated with Harlon Pease to publish a method for determining EPN, ethyl-p-nitrophenylthionobenzene phosphonate, in plant tissues by flame-ionization gas chromatography."

I rubbed my chin. "EPN? I've never heard of it before."

He smiled. "It's a pesticide."

"Where was the article published?"

"In the *Journal of Agricultural and Food Chemistry*." He paused. "If you're interested, we could send you copies of some articles published by Du Pont scientists in the past few years."

I told him I was.

Dr. Reynard then told me about the Experimental Station, and he concluded by asking if I'd like to visit Wilmington at a future date.

Sometime later I got a letter from Dr. Reynard inviting me to come to Wilmington to visit the Industrial and Biochemicals Department for further interviews. He also sent me several articles as he had promised.

One of the articles described a chromatographic method for determining Trysben (2,3,6-trichlorobenzoic acid) and Zobar (polychlorinated benzoic acid) herbicides in soil and plant tissue residues. The method consisted of extracting the unknown with MEK (methyl ethyl ketone), esterifying the acid with diazomethane

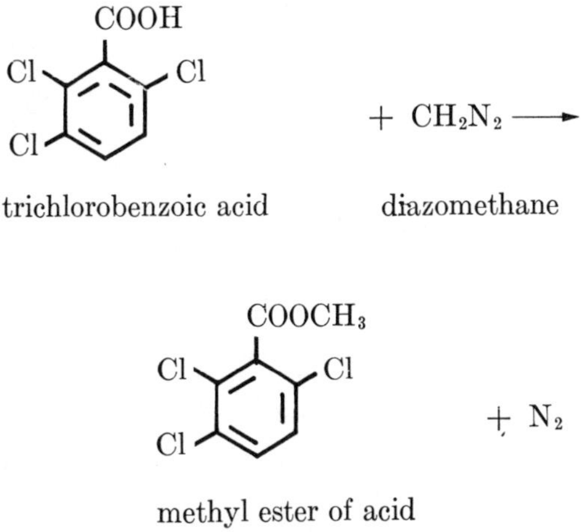

trichlorobenzoic acid   diazomethane

$$+ CH_2N_2 \longrightarrow$$

(8.1)

methyl ester of acid

$$+ N_2$$

(as shown above), and determining the presence of the ester chromatographically (Figure 30). The authors claimed that the method was sensitive to 0.04 ppm. But the article that intrigued me the most was one written by J. J. Kirkland on the use of fibrillar boehmite as a gas chromatographic support.

Baymal colloidal alumina consists of fibrous particles 50 A in diameter and about 1000 A long (A = angstrom, $1/10$ nanometer, $1/10,000$ micron, or $1/10^7$ millimeters). Because of its large surface area (ca. 275 m^2/g) and large pore volume (space between particles) this

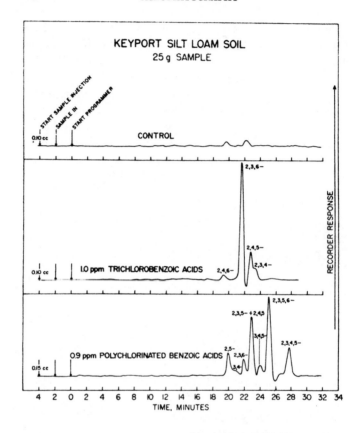

Journal of Agricultural and Food Chemistry

Fig. 30. Gas chromatograms of Keyport silt loam soil control and fortified with trichlorobenzoic and polychlorinated benzoic acids (5).

alumina has unique properties as an adsorbent in gas chromatographic columns. As received, the alumina has a surface of acetate groups, but these can be replaced by other anions, thus giving the alumina built-in specificity. Different surfaces will adsorb different things.

Baymal can be dispersed in water to form a colloidal solution. In such solutions the alumina particles have a high positive charge, and, because of the charge, the fibrils will deposit on negative surfaces such as glass, silica, ground fire brick, or diatomaceous earth. The surface thus produced will, in turn, provide an anchor for negatively charged colloidal particles, or anions, including colloidal silica, organic acids, negatively charged dyes, and many anionic surface-active agents. By such reactions one can modify inert supports in many ways. For example, glass beads can be treated alternately with a colloidal solution of fibrous alumina and colloidal silica. In this way a porous surface can be created with tailor-made pore sizes—by using colloidal silica sols having different-sized particles. For example, glass beads given five alumina–silica treatments increase in surface area from 0.02 to 0.5 m^2/g (Figures 31 and 32). Using a col-

Fig. 31. The surface of an untreated glass bead. The surface is relatively smooth; surface area is relatively low.

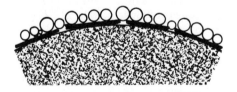

Fig. 32. The surface of a glass bead treated with fibrous alumina (depositing a monolayer of fibrous particles on the bead) and then with a colloidal silica sol (depositing a monolayer of tiny, spherical silica particles). The alumina and silica particles provide considerable new surface for adsorption reactions.

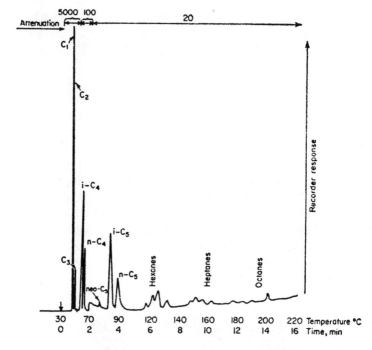

Gas Chromatography

Fig. 33. Separation of the components of natural gas by gas chromatography. The column was packed with glass beads treated with fibrous alumina and colloidal silica (*see* Fig. 32). Natural gas is mostly methane (CH_4), but it also contains small amounts of higher hydrocarbons (ethane C_2H_6, propane C_3H_8, *n*-butane C_4H_{10}, isobutane, etc.) (*4*).

umn of 60–80 mesh glass beads treated with alumina and 100 nm silica, Kirkland was able to separate natural gas into its components (Figure 33).

Capillary tubes are sometimes used in gas chromatography. It is possible to coat the internal wall of these continuously and evenly and thereby avoid the heterogeneity which is sometimes troublesome in packed columns. Capillary tubing can be made from nylon, copper, and other metals. The tubing can be wound in a coil, for example, around the outer container of a flame-ionization detector. One of the advantages of capillary columns is that analyses are possible in less than 10 minutes.

Fibrillar alumina will deposit on the internal wall of a capillary. Such a surface will, in turn, accept the nega-

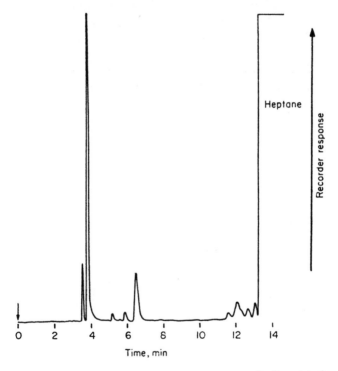

Gas Chromatography

Fig. 34. Analysis of low-boiling impurities in *n*-heptane using coated glass capillary. Sample: 0.1 1 spectral-grade *n*-heptane. Column: 300-ft, 0.02-inch id, Pyrex glass capillary, fibrillar boehmite-modified, silica sol coated. Temperature: 27°C. Detector: hydrogen flame ionization. Carrier: 12.5 cc/min helium. Split: 27:1 (*6*).

tively charged materials, indicated above. With such a column, coated with alumina and silica layers, Kirkland was able to identify low-boiling impurities in spectral-grade *n*-heptane (Figure 34).

As I read the papers, I realized there were many things about gas chromatography that I did not really understand, like theoretical plates and retention volume. It occurred to me that I might be questioned on any phase of chromatography during my major examination, or the subject might come up when I went before the committee at the university to defend my thesis, so I decided to learn more about it. After that, I spent several afternoons in the library reviewing the physical–chemical principles on which GLC is based.

Chapter 9

Separation

In my first column experiment I determined the anion exchange capacity of Amberlite IR–4B for perrhenic acid. First, I converted 5 grams of Amberlite IR–4B to the chloride form by passing a large excess of dilute hydrochloric acid through a column of resin:

$$RNH_2 + H^+ + Cl^- \longrightarrow RNH_3Cl$$

I then washed the column with several liters of water to get rid of the excess hydrochloric acid, testing the effluent for chloride with silver nitrate:

$$Cl^- + Ag^+ \longrightarrow AgCl \downarrow$$

After the liquid in the column was free of chloride, I exchanged the chloride on the resin for perrhenate by passing ammonium perrhenate, NH_4ReO_4, through the column:

$$RNH_3Cl + ReO_4^- \longrightarrow RNH_3ReO_4 + Cl^-$$

I collected 1000 ml of effluent in a 1-liter volumetric flask and then tested the next 100 ml of effluent for chloride. Finding essentially none, I assumed that the perrhenate had completely replaced the chloride in the column and that by analyzing the effluent for chloride, I would know how much perrhenate was held in the column.

I found that it required 24.5 ml of $0.053N$ AgNO$_3$ to titrate the chloride in 100 ml of effluent. From this data

I calculated the anion exchange capacity for perrhenate to be 4.4 milliequivalents per gram of dry resin.

If there were other anions present besides perrhenate, each of these would compete for adsorption, and the amount of perrhenic acid adsorbed would be less than it would be if perrhenic acid were the only acid present. In addition, if the effluent solution is passed through the column faster than the ions therein can be adsorbed, the capacity of the resin will be only partly used. Because of these factors I decided to measure the breakthrough capacity that I could expect if a solution containing perrhenic and sulfuric acids were ion exchanged.

In the breakthrough experiment, I passed a solution containing $4.2 \times 10^{-4}N$ $HReO_4$ and $2.8 \times 10^{-5}N$ H_2SO_4 through a column of 5 grams of wet resin (59% solids). Rhenium appeared in the effluent after 1050 ml of the solution had entered the column. From this I calculated the breakthrough capacity as 0.15 milliequivalent of perrhenic acid per gram of dry resin.

This corresponds to about 30 mg of rhenium adsorbed per gram of dry resin before breakthrough.

I next wrote down a standard procedure for running my column experiments:

- In each experiment use a fresh charge of resin.
- Soak the resin for at least 12 hours in distilled water.
- Treat the column with a 5% solution of sodium hydroxide, passed downflow through the column at 1.5 ml per minute.
- Backwash the column at such a rate as to cause a 50% increase in bed volume, the backwash of distilled water being introduced at the bottom of the column through the side arm of a T tube. Continue backwashing until the effluent from the top of the column is neutral to phenol red; pack the column by rapid downflow drainage.

Form a chromatogram by passing the solution containing the $HReO_4$, H_2MoO_4, and H_2SO_4 downflow through the column.

Develop the chromatogram.

Elute the adsorbates remaining after development; use 5% sodium hydroxide as the eluting agent.

I checked my procedure against the one recommended by Rohm and Haas in its "Laboratory Guide." I thought that I was ready to start, until I remembered that I hadn't selected a developing agent.

Based on my reading and batch experiments, I knew that developing agents for Amberlite IR–4B could be divided into two classes; those which caused a species to migrate because of anion exchange, and those which preferentially eluted one species. The rate of migration of any band will vary with the pH of the developing solution and the nature of the adsorbed anion, A^-. Although high pH favors rapid migration, it does not follow that this condition is the most effective for separating chromatographic bands. The effectiveness of a developing agent can be enhanced by buffering the solution at the optimum pH, the pH at which there is the greatest difference in the adsorbability of the various species.

I decided to rely on preferential elution to develop the perrhenate–molybdate chromatogram. At pH 7–8 there is little tendency for molybdate to be adsorbed, whereas rhenium is almost completely adsorbed. Since a mixture of boric acid and sodium borate can be used to prepare buffers at this pH, I decided to use a borate buffer as the developing agent.

I was extremely careful in that first experiment. I soaked 10 grams of resin in distilled water, treated it with hydroxide, and backwashed the column. I formed a chromatogram by passing 500 ml of solution containing perrhenic, molybdic, and sulfuric acids through the column at 2 ml per minute.

One thing I neglected to do was to calculate just how long it would take to form the chromatogram and develop it. At 2 ml/min it would take almost 4 hours just to form the chromatogram, and by the time I was ready to start it was already 10:30. I decided to wait until after lunch to begin.

"Well," said Mary as I met her on the way home for lunch, "how did it work out?"

I looked up at the sky and thought hard, trying to think of a way to explain it to her. "It takes longer to get started . . . I mean, when you pass a solution through a column at 2 milliliters a minute you only get 120 ml an hour."

She looked at me as if to say, good, you can multiply. "So?"

"So I'm going to start this afternoon."

"Oh."

There really wasn't much to do that afternoon while the chromatogram was being formed, so I wandered down the hall to find someone to talk to. I was gone longer than I'd expected. When I got back, the rubber stopper that I had used to attach the inlet tube to the top of the column had slipped out, the column had run dry, and most of the solution had run out on the bench top. I looked at the clock; it was almost three. In disgust, I dumped the resin from the buret into the trashcan and threw the solutions into the sink without even analyzing them.

I didn't have the heart to start another experiment that afternoon. It was one of those bright sunshiny days in early spring. The sky was full of billowy clouds, with patches of white against a background of deep blue. We had bought a Kodak with Mary's most recent paycheck, so I spent the rest of the afternoon wandering around the university campus taking color pictures. I must have tramped over the hillsides of the campus for 2 hours, taking pictures of the carillon tower and the dormitories by the lake and the university buildings. I ended up along the waterfront of Lake Mendota taking pictures of canoers. In the very late afternoon I returned to the malting laboratory where Mary was completing her afternoon's work.

She could tell right away that something had happened. "And where have you been all day?" she asked. I told her.

The next morning, I made up a fresh solution of perrhenate and molybdate, and I prepared another column with fresh resin. I didn't leave the lab all morning, and by noon the perrhenate and molybdate feed was exhausted. I had just started the developing solution when Mary came into the lab.

"Time for lunch," she announced.

"Just a minute," I said, "I'm going to wire this stopper on so it can't slip out."

I must have been in too much of a hurry when I did it because when I returned the column was dry again. At first I couldn't figure out why. And then I saw. In wiring the stopper, I had tipped it, which allowed the air to leak into the column and which relieved the partial vacuum, and allowed liquid to run out faster than it ran in.

For a long time I just stood there and looked at it. I wondered if I could recover the experiments by flooding the column with water. I tried it, but there were still air pockets, so once again I hurled the resin into the trashcan in disgust.

I started a third experiment the next day. When I came back from lunch, everything was still going as planned. By 4 o'clock I had passed about 700 ml of developing solution through the column, and no trace of perrhenate had appeared. I made a quick calculation: about 80% of the molybdate had been recovered in the effluent. I was elated.

The upper portion of the wall between my lab and the adjoining one was frosted glass. As I was pouring more developing solution into the flask, Luke, the student in the next lab, could see my reflection as I stood on the bench top. To play a joke, he pulled a yardstick across the roughened surface of the glass. It made an eerie noise.

I was so startled that I dropped the beaker and upset the column. I was furious. By this point, I was so uptight that I walked into Luke's lab, picked up his research notebook, and slammed it into the trashcan.

Table 5.   The Chromatographic Separation of Perrhenate and Molybdate with Amberlite IR–4B

Developing Agent: 0.1N Boric Acid and 0.017N Sodium Hydroxide, pH 8.35

Solutions Passed through Column:

500	ml	perrhenate–molybdate
250	ml	distilled water
2,700	ml	developing agent
50	ml	distilled water
100	ml	eluting agent—5% NaOH solution

Fraction of Effluent, ml	Molybdate Recovered, millimoles	Perrhenate Recovered, micromoles	pH of Effluent
Percolate			
750	17.62	0.0	5.18
250	1.90	0.0	7.05
250	1.73	0.0	7.55
250	1.14	0.0	7.92
250[a]	0.78	0.0	8.09
250	0.63	0.0	8.12
250	0.42	0.0	8.18
250[a]	0.43	0.0	8.18
250	0.31	0.0	8.20
500	0.42	0.0	8.30
250	0.13	0.5	
Eluant	0.45	125.0	
Total	25.96	125.5	

[a] Passage of developing solution interruption for several hours.

The next day was Saturday, another beautiful, inviting, spring day. I wanted to go back to the lab, and I would have except Gaurth and Anna Lou came over to our apartment and convinced Mary that we should go on a picnic with them. Ordinarily days such as those, when married students got together for a day of fun, were as welcome as an oasis in a desert, but on this particular day, I wasn't in the mood for a picnic. I couldn't get my research out of my mind. I managed to forget the thermos, so we didn't have anything to drink, and I didn't wear a sweater and nearly froze on the way home. To top it off, when the others suggested that we go to a movie that evening, I discovered that I'd left my wallet in my other pants. But what made me most out of sorts was that Mary was so patient and understanding through it all.

I started the fourth experiment Monday morning. By noon the chromatogram was formed, by late afternoon I'd passed several hundred ml of developing solution through the column, and so far no perrhenate had broken through. When I went out for dinner I shut off the flow of developing solution, just in case. I came back that night and stayed till almost midnight. When I finally went home, over 90% of the molybdate had been washed through the column, with no perrhenate breakthrough. The next day I passed another 750 ml of developing solution through the column, and finally I detected perrhenate. A summary of the experiment appears in Table 5.

CHAPTER 10

Defense of My Thesis

After that first successful chromatographic separation of perrhenate and molybdate, I ran several other experiments to scout a variety of developing agents, and meanwhile the summer slipped by.

In late August, I learned of a vacancy on the staff of the University of Utah. I applied for and received the appointment. The question was: if I left Wisconsin, would I have a problem completing my Ph.D.?

Mary and I talked it over. We decided that we wanted to go but felt we must have the approval of Professor Meloche before we made a final decision.

One afternoon as I was working in my lab, I heard footsteps coming into the room. It was the professor. "Hello," he said. He walked over to the door at the fire escape and looked out over the campus.

I asked him about Mrs. Meloche and we talked about baseball and his summer up north in Wisconsin. Finally I said, "I think I know how to separate rhenium and molybdenum."

He smiled, "How did you do that?"

"Remember that ion exchange resin that Professor Matthews gave me?"

He nodded.

"Well," I paused to organize my thoughts. "I've done it chromatographically. Perrhenate is more strongly adsorbed than molybdate, so you can wash all the molybdate out of an ion exchange column containing the two."

110

I showed him my graphs and the data in Table VII. "Think that would do . . . that is . . . Is this okay for my thesis?" I asked.

Again he smiled. He did not answer my question directly, but I felt he at least had approved, and if he approved, the committee was apt to approve.

"There is a vacancy on the teaching staff at the University of Utah," I said. "They need someone this fall."

"Are you interested?" He scratched his chin.

"Yes."

"Well, then I guess you'd better go."

"I would like to, sir," I paused. "There's the matter of the thesis." Again I paused. "Would it be all right with you if I wrote it up while I was teaching?"

"Could be risky." He walked back over to the window. "Luke never did finish his thesis after he left. Seems like a lot of work for nothing. Are you sure you'd finish it? This is most important for your future; you must remember that."

"Yes, sir!" I said it will all the emphasis I could.

"When?"

"By winter," I paused to see his reaction. "I could come back next spring to take my final exam." I cleared my throat. "To defend my thesis, that is, sir, if you had approved it before then."

"Well then, I guess you've already decided. Be sure to talk to me about the organization of the thesis before you go."

"Sir," I said slowly. "Do you think what I've done is satisfactory for a thesis for a Ph.D.? I don't want to leave Wisconsin if you are not satisfied with my research."

The professor smiled again. "It depends partly on how well you write it. If you really want that teaching job, you'd better go after it. I think I could approve the thesis material."

I went home and told Mary about my talk with the professor and we finally made the decision to move to Utah and write up the thesis there.

It took some time to adjust to our new life. I was assigned to a beginning class in chemistry to teach freshman engineering students. Preparing for this required more time than I had anticipated. Facilities at the University of Utah were overcrowded. There was not sufficient laboratory space for my students; we had to arrange makeshift lockers to house their equipment, and we had to run laboratories in the evening and early morning hours. I was responsible for organizing these laboratory sessions as well as instruction in lecture and quiz sections. Besides this, Mary and I had the problem of finding an apartment. Because of all the returning service men, apartments were very scarce. Late in the fall, the university brought to the campus some temporary housing which had been used for evacuated Japanese civilians, and by Christmas we were able to move into one of these units.

In this atmosphere, it was difficult for me to write my thesis. It was March before I completed the first draft. While waiting for Professor Meloche to approve it, I used the carbon copy to write several papers which I hoped we might publish in the chemical journals. I mailed these to the professor in April.

The date of my final examination, the defense of my thesis, was set for early June. By the first of May, I had not yet received any word from the professor either with regard to the thesis or the papers, so one afternoon I telephoned him. A few days later I received a package from Wisconsin. When I opened it I found to my disappointment that it was a copy of the papers I had sent to the professor.

The professor had used a blunt, red, wax pencil to make his corrections on the papers, and as I leafed through them I noticed that many of the suggestions had to do with form. Finally it dawned on me that the professor had mistaken the papers for the thesis. I was faced with a problem: should I simply recopy the thesis from the carbons, or should I try to revise and rewrite the papers in a form which would be acceptable as a thesis?

I decided on the latter course of action. Between getting the thesis rewritten and retyped, the graphs drawn and pasted in place, the whole proofread and reread, Mary and I were frustrated and nervous, and hardly speaking courteously to each other by the time I mailed the finished manuscript, just one week before the defense date.

The afternoon that I arrived in Madison, Professor Meloche was occupied and unable to see me, so he made an appointment for the next day at 10 o'clock; the examination was scheduled for that afternoon at 3. Meanwhile, I still had the two copies of the thesis for the university library. The professor was supposed to sign these, and I was supposed to deposit them in the library prior to the examination.

The next morning when I arrived at his office, the professor said he still hadn't read the thesis so how could he approve it. After considerable fumbling, we found the package containing the manuscript in the mail box.

I sat on the edge of my chair waiting for him to comment as he read through it. He said nothing. He seemed only to scowl as he picked up his red wax pencil. I sank back in despair.

Finally he looked up. "Seems in order to me," he said.

I sank back in relief, and as I did I noticed a book on atomic energy on his desk. My mind went back more than a year to the time I sat in that very office writing my preliminary examination. It was just after the ending of the war, and interest in atomic energy was still at a peak. The first question on my examination had been to discuss the principles which made an atomic bomb possible.

All of a sudden my hands went hot and cold and sweaty all at once. In less than 5 hours I would be in another examination, this one for all the marbles. In the pressure to finish the thesis and fly to Madison, I had completely forgotten to study for it. It had been a year since I had done any reading or thinking about chromatography, and this was sure to be the subject of much of the questioning during the examination that afternoon.

I don't remember saying goodbye as I left the professor's office. I felt such an urgency to review some of the things I'd learned about chromatography that I ran to the main library, deposited the signed thesis, and raced back to the chemical library in the chemistry building.

As always happens, I met a fellow graduate student, Gaurth. He'd been among my closest friends.

The fraternity of graduate students is closeknit. Of all the friends I've ever had, the ones I've been nearest to were the ones I had during graduate school in Wisconsin.

I've wondered why since. Maybe it's because of the common purpose, or the fact that we had little money so we had to find common low-cost pleasures, like a picnic on the lake shore, or a walk through the campus, or ping-pong at the student union. Maybe it's because you're doing what you like to do, taking only those subjects in school that you want to take, the ones that are a challenge, the ones that are fun, so everything and everybody looks good. Maybe it's because you're in-between; you no longer have the problems and restrictions of an adolescent, you have escaped at last into a world of your own, and yet the heavy strain of parenthood and leadership in the community or church have not yet descended on you, so you have more time for friendships.

I knew when I saw Gaurth that I might as well forget studying, at least till after lunch.

It was 1 o'clock when I got back to the chemistry library, less than two hours to review.

When the bell rang at 3, my throat was dry and the palms of my hands clammy. I went to the room where the examination was scheduled. Professor Meloche and Professor Hall from chemistry and Professor Ragatz from chemical engineering were waiting for me.

At first it was all small talk, and I relaxed with the feeling that maybe I'd get off easy. Then Professor Hall leaned back in his chair and said, "Your thesis was on chromatography?"

I nodded.

"Let's suppose," he continued, "that we have an ideal solution containing two components. Let's further assume that each of these components can be distributed between a stationary phase and a moving phase and that the concentration in one phase has a direct, linear relationship to the concentration in the other phase. Let's

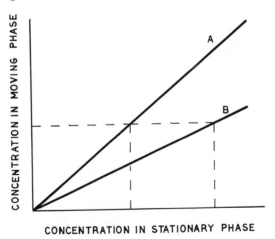

Fig. 35. Linear isotherm

assume that the exchange process is reversible, that equilibrium is immediate, and that diffusion in the phases can be ignored. Now describe, with sketches on the blackboard, what would happen if you attempted a chromatographic separation of these two components in such a system."

I drew a deep breath. It sounded simple enough, but I wanted to be sure that I didn't stumble so I started out slowly.

First I drew a graph representing the partition of the two components in the two phases (Figure 35).

"For a given concentration of either component in the moving phase," I said, "there will be a higher concentration of component B in the stationary phase."

I drew a horizontal dotted line on the figure and extended it until it intersected lines A and B. At the points of intersection, I dropped a perpendicular to the x axis.

I paused and looked up at the clock. 3:25. "Let us suppose," I continued, "that the presence of A does not affect the partition of B and *vice versa*."

Professor Hall nodded.

"If a chromatogram is formed by introducing a solution of A and B into a column, it will look like this."

I sketched another drawing on the blackboard (Figure 36). "In this discussion I assume that there are about equal concentrations of A and B in the initial solution. Because B is more strongly adsorbed in the stationary phase, the band of B will be narrow relative to the band of A. I have drawn the band of B cross-hatched to the right and A to the left. At the top of the column, the two bands overlap, with band A extending below band B.

"If pure solvent is passed through the column, the two bands will travel at different rates, band A moving more rapidly than B. After a time the two bands will only partly overlap."

I sketched Figure 37.

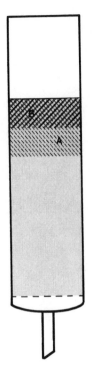

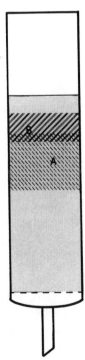

Fig. 36. Chromatogram of two solutes, A and B, each fed at the same concentration. B is more strongly adsorbed.

Fig. 37. Partially developed chromatogram. B moves more slowly than A.

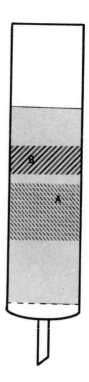

Fig. 38. Developed chromatogram.
Bands are separated.

"Eventually, if the column is long enough, the two bands will be separated."

I sketched Figure 38.

"Fine," said Professor Hall with a smile. "Now tell me, after the bands are separated what will their respective widths be, relative to their initial widths?"

"Under the conditions imposed," I said confidently, "the bands will maintain constant width as they move down the column and the boundaries will remain sharp and distinct."

Professor Meloche smiled, and I gained more confidence. This, I thought, is a snap.

"I see," said Professor Hall. "Now list for me, on the board, the conditions that are required if the bands are to remain a constant size and shape."

I made the list.

Ideal Chromatograph

1. Linear isotherm
2. Ideal solutions
3. Reversible exchange
4. Immediate equilbrium
5. No effect on partition coefficient of B by A's presence, and *vice versa*
6. No longitudinal diffusion

I paused and looked at the blackboard. "I guess these are all the conditions."

"Now," said Professor Hall, "in your studies with Amberlite IR–4B, how did that system differ from the ideal system you have just described?"

I gulped. From the grin on Professor Hall's face, I suspected he was leading me into a corner.

"Suppose we talk about a perrhenic acid–molybdic acid system and resin in the hydroxide form." I paused for approval.

Professor Hall nodded.

"First of all, the isotherms are not linear. Secondly, the solutions that I used were dilute, but they were not ideal. Next, exchange is reversible, but equilibrium is not immediate. Another difference, the presence of $HReO_4$ does affect the amount of H_2MoO_4 that can be adsorbed; hence the presence of one does affect the distribution of the other. Finally, as in the ideal case, I suspect there is little, if any, longitudinal diffusion."

"All right," said the professor, "Now, qualitatively, how does this affect the chromatogram formed?"

I had thought about this question many times. "Well, for one thing," I paused to double check my thoughts, "the boundaries of the bands will not be sharp, and as the bands move down the column they will tend to spread, particularly the trailing boundary."

The professor nodded. "Why?"

I rubbed my hands down the sides of my pants so that the chalk wouldn't slip because of the sweat. "Well . . . the isotherms for adsorption of perrhenate and molybdate are not linear. This will make the trailing edge spread." I paused and looked up at the list. "Equilibrium is probably not immediate . . . yes, it will take time for the ions to diffuse into and out of the resin particles . . . and . . . a . . . the presence of perrhenate affects . . . what I mean is the resin has a fixed capacity so that when one site exchanges perrhenate . . . takes on a perrhenate ion in place of a hydroxide, then that site cannot be occupied by molybdate, and *vice versa*. These effects will tend to cause both boundaries to be diffuse, particularly the leading edge on formation of the chromatogram and the trailing edge during development."

Professor Hall glanced up at the clock. 3:40. "Let's change the subject," he said. "Tell me, what is gel-permeation chromatography?"

I looked down at the floor and walked across the front of the room. My mind seemed blurred. "It's a . . ." I paused, a long painful pause. "It's a liquid–solid chromatographic technique," I said deliberately. "Molecules of different sizes diffuse into pores of solids with greater or lesser ease depending on the size of the molecules." My lips were dry. I licked them. "Using this principle, one can use gel-permeation chromatography to estimate molecular weights." I took a deep breath. This was getting rough.

Professor Hall scratched his head. "What's electrophoresis?"

One of the students in physical chemistry had done a Ph.D. thesis in electrophoresis. I knew the professor knew I knew the answer to this question. "Briefly, electrophoresis is the migration of charged particles under the influence of an electric field."

"List on the board," he said, "the factors which control the rate of movement."

I made a list:

1. Sign of the charges, positive or negative
2. Number of charges per particle
3. Size of the particle
4. Applied voltage
5. Distance between electrodes
6. Length of time current is applied

"I guess that's all I can think of," I said.

There was a long pause, and I squirmed internally, wondering if I'd left out something that the professor had in mind.

"Explain," he said finally, "how you might combine electrophoresis with chromatography."

I glanced up at the ceiling and then at the clock. 3:45. Chromatography and electrophoresis. I'd read an article once. I tried to remember what it was about. Gaurth and I had talked about it. It was over a year ago. It must have been in biochemistry. Amino acids? Yes, that was it.

"I read an article once," I said. I paused and scratched my head. "It had to do with separating amino acids. It was a method for combining paper chromatography with electrophoresis. Electrodes were attached to opposite sides of the paper and the chromatogram was developed by liquid flow through the paper at right angles to the electric field."

I drew a sketch on the blackboard (Figure 39).

"Is it necessary to apply the two driving forces simultaneously?" he asked.

"No."

"Let's assume," said the professor, "that we have a solution containing four compounds. One and two travel

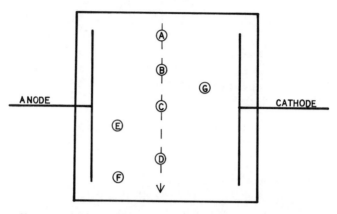

Fig. 39. Electrophoresis and chromatography. Amino acids can be separated vertically by chromatography, because of partition chromatography, and horizontally according to their electrical mobility. A, B, C, and D represent uncharged species, separated chromatographically; E and F are negatively charged species separated from A, B, C, and D by their negative charge and from each other by chromatographic mobility. G is the only positively charged species in the mixture.

Fig. 40. Paper chromatogram. Dotted circle shows position of original spot.

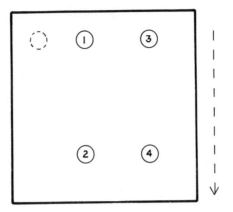

Fig. 41.   Chromatogram, followed by electrophoresis; two-dimensional separation.

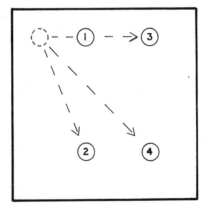

Fig. 42.   Simultaneous chromatography and electrophoresis. The final effect is the same as the final effect when the chromatograph is followed by electrophoresis. However, the path of movement is different (diagonal) for compounds 2 and 4.

together in a given paper chromatographic technique as do three and four. One and three are uncharged whereas two and four are positively charged. Show how these compounds might be separated."

Although he didn't say so, I knew he meant by combining electrophoresis and chromatography. I drew two graphs on the board (Figure 40 and 41). "At the outset, a spot of the solution is applied to paper, and the spot developed chromatographically." I pointed to the first figure. "Then an electric current is applied at right angles and compounds two and four move away from the spots formed chromatographically."

I stood back and looked at the drawings. "There is an easier and quicker way," I said. "We can apply the spot as before and simultaneously develop it chromatographically and electrophoretically. The end result will be the same, but the paths of travel will be different. Compounds 2 and 4 will move diagonally (Figure 42).

The professor smiled, "Why?"

"There are two forces acting at right angles to each other on these two compounds. The net result is that the compounds move diagonally."

He smiled again.

"One final question," he said. "What is the retardation factor?"

Once again, the abrupt change of subject unsettled me. I wanted to appear calm. Retardation, I thought, must be related to . . . What is retarded? My hands were sweaty again. Long minutes of silence.

The professor shifted nervously in his chair and scowled. He was about to say something when I asked, "You mean as related to gas chromatography?" My question was a guess, a chance to stall for time.

"Yes, certainly," he said. "Although it has been used in liquid–liquid partition. And in other contexts."

"It is . . . I think it . . . it relates to the rate at which a sample moves through a chromatographic column. Doesn't it tell how much the sample is retarded in rate?"

The professor nodded. I vaguely remembered reading about it in a textbook on gas chromatography.

I wrote an equation on the board:

$$R = \frac{T_G}{T_S}$$

"In the equation," I said, "R is the retardation factor, T_G is the time it takes the carrier gas to pass through the column, and T_S is the time it takes for the sample."

I looked up at the clock. It was almost 4 o'clock and the other two members of the committee hadn't asked me any questions, yet. At this rate, I figured, we'd be there another 2 hours.

But that wasn't the way it happened. Professor Ragatz asked a couple of questions about a class I'd taken from him in chemical engineering and then nodded to Professor Meloche that he had nothing further. Professor Meloche had no questions. He just asked me to step outside while the committee discussed their feelings. I left the room and headed for the drinking fountain.

I was about to return when I saw Professor Meloche coming toward me down the hallway. He extended his hand and said, "Congratulations, Dr. Alexander."

I stood there for a time as if frozen, in a trance. All sorts of things were racing through my mind. I would be wealthy, of course, and famous, and the rest of my life I would walk around with a sort of special radiance. I would be distinguished, a lecturer of renown, sought by all the technical societies. It would be glamorous. Maybe some day I would even win the Nobel prize, have my name in all the papers, and all the big universities would offer me all sorts of jobs.

Professor Ragatz closed the door to the classroom where I had taken the examination. All at once I was back in the real world. The committee left. I walked slowly to the front door of the chemistry building and stood there alone on the front steps.

They were the same steps I had climbed for the first time many, many months before. There had been students all around then, with the usual hustle and bustle and talk and confusion. Now the students had gone home for the summer. I thought back over what had happened —our first day in Wisconsin, the seminars, the letter from Rohm and Haas, a thesis problem, and how lucky I had been to have a major professor like Meloche who let me develop in my own way. But this was past now and my mind switched to the future and I began to wonder what kind of job I would have and where I would be in a year or two. I got all mixed up inside and a little scared.

My days at school were over. Now I must find a new goal. It was sort of like a little bird that had just learned to fly, being chased out of the nest, but not exactly like that either. After all, why should I be afraid of the world?

Theory of Gas–Liquid Chromatography

In any liquid, dissolved volatile components exert a vapor pressure above the liquid. This vapor pressure is directly proportional to the concentration of the component in the solution and to the vapor pressure of the pure component. This relationship can be expressed mathematically as follows:

$$p_a = \gamma_a x_a p_a^{\circ} \tag{A.1}$$

where p_a is the vapor pressure of component a over the solution, x_a is the mole fraction of component a in the solution, p_a° is the vapor pressure of a, the pure component, at the temperature of the solution, and γ_a is the activity coefficient of the component in the solution.

In ideal solutions, $\gamma = 1$. In an ideal binary mixture (a solution containing two components, x_1 and x_2), the relationship becomes:

$$p_1 = x_1 p_1^{\circ}$$

$$p_2 = x_2 p_2^{\circ} = (1 - x_1) p_2^{\circ}$$

The last equality is true because the sum of the mole fractions of the two components equals unity, i.e., $x_1 + x_2 = 1$.

The total vapor pressure of the solution p is the sum of the vapor pressures of the components, i.e.,

$$p = p_1 + p_2 \tag{A.2}$$

This is Raoult's law. It is plotted in Figure 43. Raoult's law is usually an oversimplification of the facts. In real

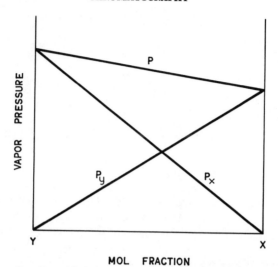

Fig. 43. Raoult's law: vapor pressures of a binary mixture where x and y are the two components of the mixture.

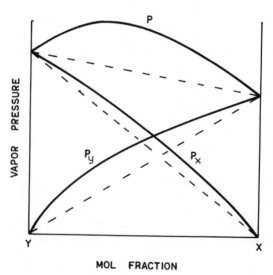

Fig. 44. Vapor pressure of a non-ideal solution, showing positive deviation from Raoult's law

cases, the more likely relationships are depicted in Figures 44 and 45.

In GLC, gas–liquid chromatography, very dilute solutions are formed when a small amount of a component from the gas stream dissolves in the liquid in the column. In such dilute solutions the dissolved molecules are so far apart that they have little, if any, attraction for each other. Thus the activity coefficients are essentially constant and approach unity (Figure 46).

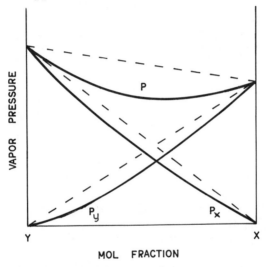

Fig. 45. Vapor pressure of a non-ideal solution, showing negative deviation from Raoult's law

The fact that there is an equilibrium in which a solute can dissolve in the stationary solvent or evaporate and exist in the mobile gas stream is the basis for separation in GLC. Experimentation has proved that the ratio of the concentration of the solute in the liquid to the concentration of the solute in the gas stream is a constant. This constant in called the partition coefficient. The mathematical relationship defining the partition coefficient K is:

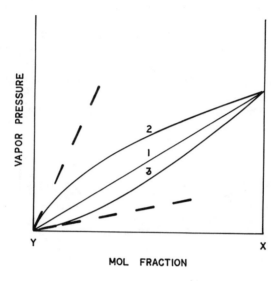

Fig. 46. Henry's Law. As shown in Figures 44 and 45, the behavior of non-ideal liquids is complicated and unpredictable. However, in the case of GLC (gas liquid chromatography) the fact that the solute molecules are present in low concentrations allows one to make a simplification. Because of their dilute solutions, the solute molecules do not exert a mutual influence on each other. In such dilute solutions the volatility (vapor pressure) of the solute is determined mainly by the intermolecular forces between the solute and solvent molecules. Henry's law is based on this fact; Henry's law states that the vapor pressure of a solute in dilute solution is proportional to its mole fraction. The solid lines in Figure 46 are taken from Fig. 43 (1 is the same as p_y in Fig. 43), Fig. 44 (2 is the p_y in Fig. 44) and Fig. 45 (3 is p_y in Fig. 45). The straight dotted lines above curve 2 and below curve 3, Fig. 46 coincide with the solid lines at low concentrations. The points of departure of the straight, dotted lines and the curved, solid lines indicate concentrations of X above which Henry's law no longer applies.

$$K = \frac{S_l}{S_g} \qquad (A.3)$$

where S_l is the weight of solute/ml of stationary liquid (mg/ml), and S_g is the weight of solute/ml of gas phase (mg/ml). Consider a small segment of a GLC column having a height, h, at the influent end of the column. If A is the cross-sectional area of the column, then the volume of this segment is hA. If h is in cm and A is in sq cm, the volume hA is in cu cm or cc. We can call this segment a theoretical plate (Figure 47).

If we examine the cross-section, we see three zones: (a) the solid support, the powder on which the liquid

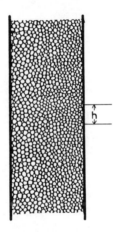

Fig. 47. A theoretical plate in a GLC column. A theoretical plate is a small segment of height, h, in the column. In a thoretical plate, the solute partitions itself between the liquid (on the solid beads) and the vapor phase according to Henry's law: $S_l = KS_g$. If the units of area and height are sq cm and cm, respectively, then the unit of volume is cc. Thus:

$$
\begin{aligned}
\text{Total cross sectional area} &= A_T \text{ sq cm} \\
\text{Height of plate} &= h \text{ cm} \\
\text{Total volume of plate} &= hA_T \text{ cc}
\end{aligned}
$$

phase is adsorbed; (b) the liquid surrounding each solid particle; and (c) the vapor or gas phase filling the voids left by the solid–liquid phase (Figures 48 and 49).

Let A_l = cross-sectional area of the liquid phase, phase 2 above, and A_g = cross-sectional area of the gas phase, phase 3.

Hence: hA_l = volume of the liquid phase, and hA_g = volume of the gas phase.

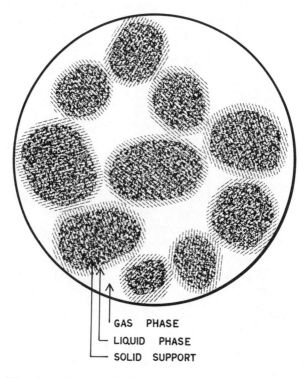

GAS   PHASE
LIQUID   PHASE
SOLID   SUPPORT

Fig. 48. Cross-sectional view of a gas-liquid chromatographic GLC column showing the three phases: (a) solid support, (b) liquid phase surrounding support, and (c) gas.

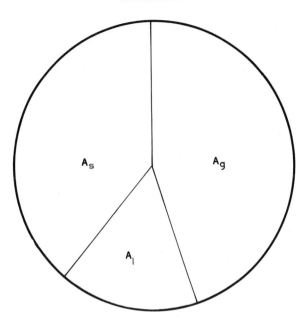

Fig. 49. Graphic representation of cross section of GLC. A_g is the cross-sectional area of the gas, A_1 of the liquid, and A_s of the solid support. Assuming that the areas are in sq cm and the height in cm, the volumes are: gas phase hA_g cc, and liquid phase hA_1 cc. Since, by definition, the volume of the gas phase in the column is Q cc/plate, then: $Q = hA_g$.

For convenience let us define:

$$hA_g = Q$$

$$hA_1 = V_1$$

Now, if S_1 is the concentration of solute in the liquid phase, e.g., mg/ml, and V_1 is the volume in ml, the total amount of solute in the liquid phase in mg is:

$$S_1 \, mg/ml \times V_1 \, ml = S_1 V_1 \, mg = S_1 h A_1 \, mg$$

and the amount in the gas phase is

$$S_g Q \text{ or } h S_g A_g \text{ mg}$$

If a unit weight of solute is added to the plate, it will partition itself such that: $h S_l A_l$ units of solute are present in the liquid phase, and $h S_g A_g$ or $Q A_g$ units of solute are present in the gas phase.

Since one unit weight was added in total,

$$h S_l A_l + h S_g A_g = 1 \qquad (A.4)$$

From Equation A.3, $S_l = K S_g$. Substituting this in Equation A.4 it becomes:

$$h K S_g A_l + h S_g A_g = 1$$

or

$$S_g [h (K A_l + A_g)] = 1 \qquad (A.5)$$

In Equation A.5, h, K, A_l, and A_g are constants; hence the quantity in the bracket is a constant. Let this quantity be E_v, i.e.,

$$E_v = h (K A_l + A_g)$$

whence:

$$S_g E_v = 1 \qquad (A.6)$$

When a carrier gas sweeps through a GLC, it carries with it the solute in the gas phase and leaves behind the solute in the liquid phase. This leaves the gas phase deficient in solute, so a new equilibrium is established by some of the solute in the liquid passing into the gas phase.

Let us now define: X_b = the fraction of the solute in a theoretical plate which is left behind when the gas moves through the plate by the gas, and X_f = the fraction of the solute which is carried forward to the next plate by the gas.

Then in the case just discussed X_b is the solute in the liquid phase:

$$X_b = hS_1A_1 \tag{A.7}$$

and if X_f is the solute in the gas phase:

$$X_f = hA_gS_g = QS_g = \frac{Q}{E_v} \tag{A.8}$$

(since from Equation A.6, $S_gE_v = 1$). Substituting this equality in Equation A.4, we obtain:

$$X_b + X_f = 1 \tag{A.9}$$

Let us assume that the gas which moves into the first plate (to replace the gas which has moved into the second plate) contains no solute. The solute left behind in the liquid phase X_b redistributes itself.

The total amount of solute is now X_b, and hence:

$$h(S_1)'A_1 + h(S_g)'A_g = X_b \tag{A.10}$$

$$hK(S_g)'A + h(S_g)' A_g = X_b \tag{A.11}$$

$$(S_g)' E_v = X_b \tag{A.12}$$

where $(S_g)'$ and $(S_1)'$ are the new concentrations of solute in the gas and liquid respectively.

When a second volume of carrier gas sweeps past the first plate, after the new equilibrium condition has been established, it carries with it $Q(S_g)'$ units of solute. But

$$(S_g)' = \frac{X_b}{E_v}$$

(from Equation A.12)

whence

$$Q(S_g)' = \frac{QX_b}{E_v}$$

From equation A.8,

$$Q/E_v = X_f$$

whence

$$Q(S_g)' = X_bX_f \tag{A.14}$$

If $Q(S_g)'$ is the amount of solute carried away from the first plate by the second volume of gas as it sweeps through the first plate, then, from the equality in Equation A.14, X_bX_f is also the amount of solute carried away in this operation.

The amount of solute left behind on the first plate after X_bX_f is carried away is the amount originally present minus that carried away, i.e.,

$$X_b - X_bX_f = X_b(1 - X_f)$$

But $(1 - X_f) = X_b$ (from Equation A.9).

Whence X_b^2 is the amount of solute left behind on the first plate after the second increment of carrier gas has passed that plate (Fig. 50).

By way of review, we added one unit weight of solute to the first plate of a GLC. This unit weight of solute partitioned itself such that X_b units were present in the liquid phase and X_f units were present in the gas phase:

$$X_b + X_f = 1$$

When a volume of gas equal to the volume of the gas phase in Plate 1 swept through the plate, all the solute in the gas phase (X_f) was swept on to Plate 2.

Since the gas phase was then devoid of solute, the solute in the liquid redistributed itself such that there

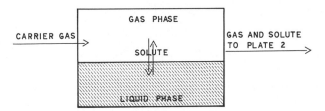

Fig. 50. Schematic of plate 1 in a gas–liquid chromatograph. Initially one unit of solute is added to this plate. This solute distributes itself between the gas and liquid phases, X_f units being present in the gas phase and X_b units in the liquid phase.

$$X_f + X_b = 1$$

When one volume of gas passes through the plate, the solute in the gas phase X_f passes on to Plate 2, leaving X_b units of solute behind. The solute left behind now redistributes itself between the gas and liquid, $X_f X_b$ units of solute being present in the gas phase and $X_b{}^2$ in the liquid phase.

$$X_f X_b + X_b{}^2 = X_b(X_f + X_b) = X_b$$

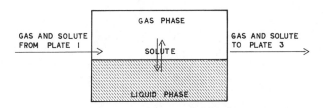

Fig. 51. Graphic representation of the equilibria in Plate 2 of a GLC after the first volume of carrier gas carrying X_f units of solute reaches the plate. This solute redistributes itself such that: $X_b X_f$ units are present in the liquid phase, and $X_f{}^2$ units are present in the gas phase.

$$X_b X_f + X_f{}^2 = X_f(X_b + X_f) = X_f$$

were X_b^2 units present in the liquid phase and X_bX_f units present in the gas phase:

$$X_b^2 + X_bX_f = X_b$$

By continuing the calculation, one can show that the solute left behind at the first plate, S_1, after n volumes of carrier gas have passed through the column is:

$$S_1 = X_b^n$$

In summary, the conditions in Plate 1 can be shown schematically in Figure 50 and Table A.1.

Table A.1.   Concentration of Solute in Plate 1

Volumes of Gas Passed through Plate	Solute Added to Plate	Total Solute Present	Solute Present in Liquid Phase	Solute Present in Gas Phase
0	1 unit	1	X_b	X_f
1	0	X_b	X_b^2	X_fX_b
2	0	X_b^2	X_b^3	$X_fX_b^2$
3	0	X_b^3	X_b^4	$X_fX_b^3$
4	0	X_b^4	X_b^5	$X_fX_b^4$
n	0	X_b^n	X_b^{n+1}	$X_fX_b^n$

The calculation with regard to Plate 2 is slightly more complex because as each volume of gas comes from Plate 1, it brings solute with it, and as the gas proceeds to Plate 3 it carries solute away. This condition is summarized schematically in Figure 51.

The calculation can be made as follows: the amount of solute arriving at the second plate in the first increment of carrier gas is X_f. A part of this solute immediately dissolves in the liquid phase in the second plate. As a result, X_f distributes itself between the gas and liquid according to the relationship

$$S_{g_2}E_v = X_f \tag{A.15}$$

where subscript 2 refers to Plate 2. This relationship is calculated by a series of steps similar to those used in Equations A.4, A.5, and A.6.

The amount of this solute which remains in the gas phase after equilibrium has been established is:

$$QS_{g_2} \text{ or } \frac{QX_f}{E_v} \text{ or } X_f^2$$

units of solute. These equalities follow from Equations A.12 and A.8. The amount of solute in the liquid phase is the total amount arriving in the increment of incoming gas minus the amount remaining in the gas phase after equilibrium with the liquid, i.e., $X_f - X_f^2$, but:

$$X_f - X_f^2 = X_f(1 - X_f) = X_f X_b$$

As this increment of carrier gas leaves Plate 2, it removes X_f^2, and as the next increment of gas arrives, it brings $X_f X_b$; hence the total amount of solute in Plate 2 is $2X_f X_b$ ($X_f X_b$ incoming plus $X_f X_b$ in the liquid phase). By continuing the calculation, one can show that the amount of solute in the second plate, S_2, after n increments of carrier gas have passed through the plate is:

$$S_2 = nX_b^{(n-1)}X_f \tag{A.16}$$

The conditions in Plate 2 are summarized in Table A.2.

Table A.2. Concentration of Solute in Plate 2

Volumes of Gas Passed through Plate	Solute Added from Plate 1	Total Solute Present	Solute in Liquid Phase	Solute in Gas Phase
1	X_f	X_f	$X_b X_f$	X_f^2
2	$X_b X_f$	$2X_b X_f$	$2X_b^2 X_f$	$2X_b X_f^2$
3	$X_b^2 X_f$	$3X_b^2 X_f$	$3X_b^3 X_f$	$3X_b^2 X_f^2$
4	$X_b^3 X_f$	$4X_b^3 X_f$	$4X_b^4 X_f$	$4X_b^3 X_f^2$
5	$X_b^4 X_f$	$5X_b^4 X_f$	$5X_b^5 X_f$	$5X_b^4 X_f^2$
n	$X_b^{n-1} X_f$	$nX_b^{n-1} X_f$	$nX_b^n X_f$	$nX_b^{n-1} X_f^2$

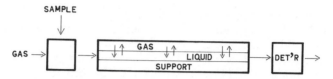

Fig. 52. Schematic of a GLC. The unknown is introduced in the carrier gas. In the column, the unknown enters and leaves the liquid many times. In so doing the components in the unknown which are "held up" longer in the liquid phase move more slowly through the column. Eventually the components of the unknown emerge from the column and are detected.

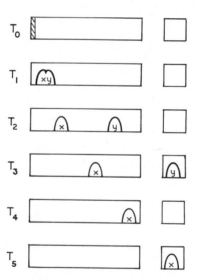

Fig. 53. Stages in the development of a GLC.

Time	Event
T_0	Carrier gas and sample introduced
T_1	Peaks begin to separate
T_2	Peaks are separated
T_3	First component emerges and is detected
T_4	Second component approaches outlet
T_5	Second component emerges and is detected

Similarly, on the third plate, after the passage of n increments of gas, the amount of solute in the plate is:

$$S_3 = \frac{n!\, X_b{}^{(n-2)} X_f}{2\,(n-2)!} \tag{A.17}$$

and on plate y:

$$S_y = \frac{n!\, X_b{}^{(n-y+1)} X_f{}^{(y-1)}}{(y-1)!\,(n-y+1)!} \tag{A.18}$$

In qualitative terms, only the solute molecules in the gas phase move; those in the liquid phase remain relatively immobile (Fig. 52). When the concentration of solute in the gas phase falls because of the movement of the gas phase, some of the solute in the liquid volatizes. The time required for a solute to pass through a column is proportional to the partition coefficient, i.e., to the ratio of the number of molecules in the liquid to those in the gas phase. The time is also related to the ratio of the cross-sectional areas of the gas and the liquid. Thus if carrier gas passes through a unit length of the column in time t, solute molecules will require a longer time, i.e., $KA_l t / A_g$, to pass through the same distance.

Now let's review what happens when a sample is introduced in a gas–liquid chromatographic column (Fig. 53). The sample is introduced at zero time (Fig. 54). Air and other components which are not adsorbed will be swept through the column and emerge as an air peak at t_A. Components which are soluble in the liquid in the column will pass through the column more slowly, the individual molecules being dissolved and vaporized many times. While they are in solution, their downward progress is interrupted as the gas passes by them. They are, in this condition, part of the X_b, the solute left behind. The solute, introduced as a unit, becomes spread into a band. This band will finally emerge, as a peak ABC, at time t_R. Time t_R is the retention time, and the volume of carrier gas required to sweep the solute through the column is the retention volume V_R.

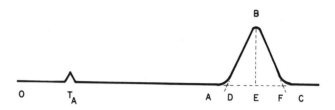

Fig. 54. Differential gas chromatogram showing the base line OAC, O being zero time, i.e., the time the sample was injected. Air and other gases introduced with the sample are swept through the column at the same speed as the carrier gas. The air peak is T_A. The retention time is the time to reach the peak maximum, i.e., T_A to B. The equivalent volume of gas is the retention volume. The peak base is AC, the interpolation of the base line and the peak. DF is the peak width, and BE the peak height.

The base line is that portion of the chromatogram when no solute is emerging from the column. The peak base AC is the extension of the base line through the bottom of the peak. The peak area is the area enclosed by the peak and the peak base, and the peak height BE is the maximum extension of the peak from the peak base. The peak width DF is the distance between the intersection of the sides of the peak with the base line.

The volume of gas originally present in the column V_C accounts for the time required to reach the air peak. This volume is equivalent to A_gL, where L is the overall length of the column. The adjusted retention volume V is defined as:

$$V = V_R - V_C \qquad (A.19)$$

It corresponds to the amount of gas which passes through the column between t_A and t_R. Specifically, V is the volume of gas required to sweep a given solute through the column.

The adjusted retention volume (like molecular weight, melting point, or refractive index) is characteristic of a given solute and hence can be used as a clue to the identification of an unknown.

The adjusted retention volume of one compound can be expressed relative to that of another compound, provided the same column is used at the same temperature:

$$R_{12} = \frac{V_1}{V_2} \qquad (A.20)$$

R_{12} is the relative retention of Compound 1 vs. Compound 2, V_1 is the adjusted retention volume of Compound 1, and V_2 of Compound 2. Note that R_{12} can be estimated from the retention volumes, V_R, provided V_C is small compared with the unadjusted retention volumes of each of the compounds.

Using certain mathematical assumptions, one can show that Equation A.15 can be written approximately as:

$$S_y = \frac{1}{\sqrt{2\pi y}} \left(\frac{nX_f}{y} \right)^y e^{(y - nX_f)} \qquad (A.21)$$

From this equation one can calculate, by differentiation, the peak height, $(S_y)_{max}$, the maximum value of S_y in the column:

$$(S_y)_{max} = \frac{1}{\sqrt{2\pi y}} \qquad (A.22)$$

This maximum occurs when the term $(y - nX_f) = 0$, or:

$$y = nX_f \qquad (A.23)$$

However, $X_f = Q/E_V$ (from Equation A.8), whence:

$$nX_f = \frac{nQ}{E_V}$$

Since n is the number of volumes of carrier gas which has passed through the column, and Q is the volume of gas/plate, nQ is the total volume of gas which has passed through the column V_R. Thus the peak maximum occurs on the yth plate where:

$$y = nX_f = \frac{nQ}{E_V} = \frac{V_R}{E_V},$$

whence:

$$V_R = yE_V \tag{A.24}$$

However, by definition, $E_V = h(A_1K + A_g)$, so:

$$V_R = yh(A_1K + A_g)$$

also, $yhA_1 = V_L$ and $yhA_g = V_G$, whence:

$$V_R = KV_L + V_G \tag{A.25}$$

The peak width W_p is given by the expression:

$$W_p = 4E_V \sqrt{y} \tag{A.26}$$

In actual experiments, one measures retention volume V_R and peak width W_p. From such observations one can estimate the number of plates in the column y by combining Equations A.24 and A.26:

$$y = 16 \left(\frac{V_R}{W_p}\right)^2 \tag{A.27}$$

Nomenclature

p_a	= vapor pressure of solute a over its solution
X_a	= mole fraction of solute a
$p_a{}^\circ$	= vapor pressure of pure a
γ_a	= activity coefficient of a
p_1	= partial pressure of Component 1
X_1	= mole fraction of Component 1
K	= partition coefficient

S_l = weight of solute in liquid per ml of liquid
S_g = weight of solute in gas per ml of gas
Q = volume of gas in each plate in the column
A_g = cross-sectional area of the gas phase in the column
A_l = cross-sectional area of the liquid phase
h = height of a theoretical plate
X_b = fraction of the solute left behind as gas sweeps through the column
X_f = fraction of the solute carried forward in the gas stream
S_1 = concentration of solute at Plate 1
y = y^{th} plate in the column
S_y = concentration of solute at Plate y
n = number of volumes of carrier gas which have passed through the column
V = adjusted retention volume, $V = V_R - V_C$
V_R = retention volume
V_C = volume of gas in the column, $V_C = A_g L$ (L = length of column)
t_R = retention time
t_A = time to the air peak
$(S_y)_{max}$ = peak height, the concentration of solute at the plate where said concentration is a maximum
W_p = peak width

Determination of the Capacity of Amberlite IR-4B

The rated capacity of Amberlite IR-4B is 25 kilograins as calcium carbonate per cubic foot. The density, as shipped, of the resin is 35 pounds per cubic foot. Hence the capacity is:

$$25 \text{ kilograins } CaCO_3/35 \text{ pounds resin}$$

but:

$$25 \text{ kilograins} = (25 \text{ kilograins}) (65 \text{ grams/kilograin}) = 1620 \text{ grams}$$

The molecular weight of $CaCO_3$ is 100. The valence of calcium is two; hence, for reactions which depend on charge (like ion exchange) there are two points of reaction in each molecule or two equivalent weights in each molecular weight. The equivalent weight of $CaCO_3$ is thus half of the molecular weight, or 50. We say: 50 grams $CaCO_3$/equivalent. Hence:

$$1620 \text{ grams } CaCO_3 = \frac{1620 \text{ grams } CaCO_3}{50 \text{ grams/equivalent}}$$

$$= 32 \text{ equivalents } CaCO_3$$

$$1 \text{ equivalent} = 1000 \text{ milliequivalents}$$

or:

$$32 \text{ equivalents } CaCO_3 = 32{,}000 \text{ milliequivalents } CaCO_3$$

Also:

$$35 \text{ pounds of resin} = (35 \text{ pounds}) (454 \text{ grams/pound}) = 15{,}900 \text{ grams resin}$$

146

whence:

25 kilograins $CaCO_3$/35 pounds resin =

32,000 milliequivalents $CaCO_3$/15,900 grams resin
or 2 milliequivalents/ gram resin (wet)

If the resin is 60% solids and 40% moisture, the capacity is 2 milliequivalents/gram of wet resin or 0.6 gram dry resin; hence the capacity is:

3.3 milliequivalents/gram dry resin.

Fractionating Column Theory

In several places throughout this book, I have referred to "theoretical plates." The term comes originally from fractionating (distillation) column theory. A short discussion of "theoretical plate" is inserted here for those interested in knowing what a theoretical plate means to a chemical engineer.

A theoretical plate is a section in an "ideal" distillation column in which the vapor leaving the plate (rising up the column) is in equilibrium with the liquid passing down the column to the plate below.

Figure 55 is the boiling point diagram for mixtures of two liquids, A and B, whose boiling points are T_A and T_B.

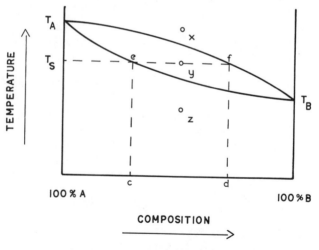

Fig. 55. Boiling point diagram

148

Liquid B has the lower boiling point, i.e., it is more volatile. Composition of the solution (mixtures of A and B) are plotted on the abscissa. The extreme left is 100% A and the extreme right 100% B. Points between contain various amounts of A and B in relation to the nearness to each component.

A solution at point c is approximately 60% A and 40% B. If this solution is heated, its temperature will increase until it reaches T_s, at which temperature the solution will boil. From the lower curve one can determine the boiling point of a solution of given composition.

The vapor formed as a result of boiling has a composition D, i.e., it is 78% B and 22% A. In other words, the vapor above the boiling solution is richer in the lower boiling component than is the solution.

Any two points on the same horizontal line which cuts both the upper and lower curves in a boiling point diagram represent the composition of the vapor (upper curve) and the composition of the liquid (lower curve) in equilibrium with each other at the temperature given by the horizontal line.

Any point, e.g. X, above the upper curve represents vapor only. Any point, e.g. Z, below the lower curve represents liquid only. Points between the two curves, e.g. Y, represent systems consisting of liquid and vapor.

As a solution of composition C is boiled, since the vapor is rich in B, the solution will tend to become rich in A, and eventually the boiling point will move upward to T_A.

Suppose a distillation column is filled with several plates, each of which is boiling. The objective of the column is to separate a solution of composition C into its pure components A and B. A theoretical plate in such a column is one in which the liquid of composition C on the plate, returning to the column below it, is in equilibrium with the vapor of composition D, rising to the plate above it.

Let us consider Plate n in the distillation column in Figure 56. This plate is involved with four streams of material: (a) a vapor rising from the plate below, Plate

$n + 1$, which condenses on plate n; (b) a vapor rising to the plate above, Plate $n - 1$; (c) a liquid from the plate above; and (d) a liquid returning to the plate below.

Let us assume that Plate n is a theoretical plate. The liquid leaving Plate n to the plate below must be in equilibrium with the vapor rising from Plate n to the plate above. For example, if Plate n is returning a liquid of composition c to plate $n + 1$ (*see* Fig. 56), the composition of the vapor rising from Plate n to Plate $n - 1$ would, by definition, have a composition d. The compositions of the other two streams, i.e., those coming to plate n, would have compositions between c and d. The compositions of the streams coming to or leaving from Plate n are shown in Figure 57.

It is evident that the liquid of composition g is not in equilibrium with vapor of composition h. When these

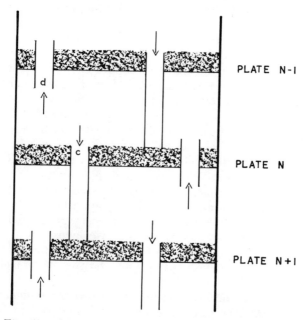

Fig. 56. Plates in the middle of a distillation column

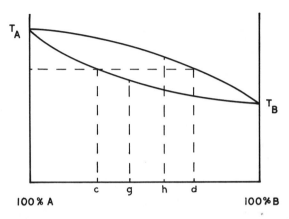

Fig. 57. Boiling point diagram where *c* is the composition of the liquid leaving for plate *n* + 1, *d* is the composition of the vapor rising to plate *n* − 1, *g* is the composition of the liquid coming to plate *n* from plate *n* − 1, and *h* is the composition of the vapor coming to plate *n* from plate *n* + 1.

two streams are brought together on Plate *n*, they release two streams, c and d, which are in equilibrium, by vaporizing some of component B in the stream g and condensing some of component A in stream h. Thus the more volatile component evaporates from the liquid stream and is carried up the column, and the less volatile component is condensed from the vapor stream and carried down the column.

If the column is long enough, i.e., has enough theoretical plates, then the liquid in the pot at the bottom of the column will approach pure A and the vapor leaving the top of the column will be pure B.

Literature Cited

1. Machata, G., *Mikrochim. Acta* (1960) 79.
2. Stahl, E., *Perfuem. + Kosmet.* (1958) **39**, 564.
3. Stanley, W. L., Vannier, S. H., *J. Assoc. Off. Anal. Chem.* (1957) **40**, 582.
4. Kirkland, J. J., "Gas Chromatography," p 289, The Institute of Petroleum, London, 1964.
5. Kirkland, J. J., Pease, H. L., *J. Agric. Food Chem.* (1964) **12**, 471.
6. Kirkland, J. J., "Gas Chromatography," p 291, The Institute of Petroleum, London, 1964.

Glossary of Ion Exchange[a]

Certain license has been taken with the strict semantic interpretation of the following words, in order to present definitions related specifically to ion exchange technology.

Acidity: An expression of the concentration of hydrogen ions present in a solution.

Adsorbent: A synthetic resin possessing the ability to attract and to hold charged particles.

Adsorption: The attachment of charged particles to the chemically active groups on the surface and in the pores of an ion exchanger.

Alkalinity: An expression of the total basic anions (hydroxyl groups) present in a solution. It also represents, particularly in water analysis, the bicarbonate, carbonate, and occasionally, the borate, silicate, and phosphate salts which will react with water to produce the hydroxyl groups.

Anion: A negatively charged ion.

Anion interchange: The displacement of one negatively charged particle by another on an anion exchange material.

Attrition: The rubbing of one particle against another in a resin bed; frictional wear that will affect the size of resin particles.

Backwash: The upward flow of water through a resin bed (i.e., in at the bottom of the exchange unit, out at the top) to clean and reclassify the bed after exhaustion.

Base-exchange: The property of the trading of cations shown by certain insoluble naturally occurring materials (zeolites) and developed to a high degree of specificity and efficiency in synthetic resin adsorbents.

Batch operation: The utilization of ion exchange resins to treat a solution in a container wherein the removal of ions is accomplished by agitation of the solution and subsequent decanting of the treated liquid.

Bed: The ion exchange resin contained in a column.

[a] Courtesy Rohm and Haas.

Bed depth: The height of the resinous material in the column after the exchanger has been properly conditioned for effective operation.

Bed expansion: The effect produced during backwashing: the resin particles become separated and rise in the column. The expansion of the bed due to the increase in the space between resin particles may be controlled by regulating backwash flow.

Bicarbonate alkalinity: The presence in a solution of hydroxyl (OH^-) ions resulting from the hydrolysis of carbonates or bicarbonates. When these salts react with water, a strong base and a weak acid are produced, and the solution is alkaline.

Breakthrough: The first appearance in the solution flowing from an ion exchange unit of unadsorbed ions similar to those which are depleting the activity of the resin bed. Breakthrough is an indication that regeneration of the resin is necessary.

Capacity: The adsorption ability possessed in varying degree by ion exchange materials. This quality may be expressed as kilograms per cubic foot, gram-milliequivalents per gram, pound-equivalents per pound, gram-milliequivalents per milliliter, etc., where the numerators of these ratios represent the weight of the ions adsorbed and the denominators, the weight or volume of the adsorbent.

Carbonaceous exchangers: Ion exchange materials of limited capacity prepared by the sulfonation of coal, lignite, peat, etc.

Carboxylic: A term describing a specific acidic group ($COOH$) that contributes cation exchange ability to some resins.

Cation: A positively charged ion.

Channeling: Cleavage and furrowing of the bed due to faulty operational procedures, in which the solution being treated follows the path of least resistance, runs through these furrows, and fails to contact active groups in other parts of the bed.

Chemical stability: Resistance to chemical change which ion exchange resins must possess despite contact with aggressive solutions.

Color-throw: Discoloration of the liquid passing through an ion exchange material; the flushing from the resin interstices of traces of colored organic reaction intermediates.

Column operation: Conventional utilization of ion exchange resins in columns through which pass, either upflow or downflow, the solution to be treated.

Cycle: A complete course of ion exchange operation. For instance, a complete cycle of cation exchange would involve: exhaustion of regenerated bed, backwash, regeneration, and rinse to remove excess regenerant.

Deashing: The removal from solution of inorganic salts by means of adsorption by ion exchange resins of both the cations and the anions that comprise the salts. See deionization.

Deionization: See deashing. Deionization, a more general term than deashing, embraces the removal of all charged constituents or ionizable salts (both inorganic and organic) from solution.

Demineralizing: See deashing.

Density: The weight of a given volume of exchange material, backwashed and in place in the column.

Dissociation: Ionization.

Downflow: Conventional direction of solutions to be processed in ion exchange column operation, i.e., in at the top, out at the bottom of the column.

Dynamic system: An ion exchange operation wherein a flow of the solution to be treated is involved.

Efficiency: The effectiveness of the operational performance of an ion exchanger. Efficiency in the adsorption of ions is expressed as the quantity of regenerant required to effect the removal of a specified unit weight of adsorbed material, e.g., pounds of acid per kilograin of salt removed.

Effluent: The solution which emerges from an ion exchange column.

Electrolyte: A chemical compound which dissociates or ionizes in water to produce a solution which will conduct an electric current; an acid, base, or salt.

Elution: The stripping of adsorbed ions from an ion exchange material by the use of solutions containing other ions in relatively high concentrations.

Equilibrium reactions: The interaction of ionizable compounds in which the products obtained tend to revert to the substances from which they were formed until a balance is reached in which both reactants and products are present in definite ratios.

Equivalent weight: The molecular weight of any element or radical expressed as grams, pounds, etc., divided by the valence.

Exchange velocity: The rate with which one ion is displaced from an exchanger in favor of another.

Exhaustion: The state in which the adsorbent is no longer capable of useful ion exchange; the depletion of the exchanger's supply of available ions. The exhaustion point is determined arbitrarily in terms of: (a) a value in parts per million of ions in the effluent solution; (b) the reduction in quality of the effluent water determined by a conductivity bridge which measures the electrical resistance of the water.

Fines: Extremely small particles of ion exchange materials.

Flow rate: The volume of solution passing through a given quantity of resin within a given time. Usually expressed in terms of gallons per minute per cubic foot of resin, as millimeters per minute per milliliter of resin, or as gallons per square foot of resin per minute.

Freeboard: The space provided above the resin bed in an ion exchange column to allow for expansion of the bed during backwashing.

Grain: A unit of weight; 0.0648 gram.

Grains per gallon: An expression of concentration of material in solution, generally in terms of calcium carbonate. One grain (as calcium carbonate) per gallon is equivalent to 17.1 parts per million.

Gram-milliequivalents: The equivalent weight in grams, divided by 1000.

Greensands: Naturally-occurring materials, composed primarily of complex silicates, which possess ion exchange properties.

Hardness: The scale-forming and lather-inhibiting qualities which water, high in calcium and magnesium ions, possesses. Temporary hardness, caused by the presence of magnesium or calcium bicarbonate, is so called because it may be removed by boiling the water to convert the bicarbonates to the insoluble carbonates. Calcium sulfate, magnesium sulfate, and the chlorides of these two metals cause permanent hardness.

Hardness as calcium carbonate: The expression ascribed to the value obtained when the hardness-forming salts are calculated in terms of equivalent quantities of calcium carbonate; a convenient method of reducing all salts to a common basis for comparison.

Headloss: The reduction in liquid pressure associated with the passage of a solution through a bed of exchange material; a measure of the resistance of a resin bed to the flow of the liquid passing through it.

Hydraulic classification: The rearrangement of resin particles in an ion exchange unit. As the backwash water flows up through the resin bed, the particles are placed in a mobile condition wherein the larger particles settle and the smaller particles rise to the top of the bed.

Hydrogen cycle: A complete course of cation exchange operation in which the adsorbent is employed in the hydrogen or free acid form.

Hydroxyl: The term used to describe the anionic radical (OH^-) which is responsible for the alkalinity of a solution.

Influent: The solution which enters an ion exchange unit.

Ion: Any particle of less than colloidal size possessing either a positive or a negative electric charge.

Ionization: The dissociation of molecules into charged particles.

Ionization constant: An expression in absolute units of the extent of dissociation into ions of a chemical compound in solution.

Kilograin: A unit of weight; one thousand grains.

Leakage: The phenomenon in which some of the influent ions are not adsorbed and appear in the effluent when a solution is passed through an under-regenerated exchange resin bed.

Negative charge: The electrical potential which an atom acquires when it gains one or more electrons; a characteristic of an anion.

pH: An expression of the acidity of a solution; the negative logarithm of the hydrogen ion concentration (pH 1, very acidic; pH 14, very basic; pH 7, neutral).

pOH: An expression of the alkalinity of a solution; the negative logarithm of the hydroxyl ion concentration.

pK: An expression of the extent of dissociation of an electrolyte; the negative logarithm of the ionization constant of a compound.

Physical stability: The quality which an ion exchange resin must possess to resist changes that might be caused by attrition, high temperatures, and other physical conditions.

Positive charge: The electrical potential acquired by an atom which has lost one or more electrons; a characteristic of a cation.

Raw water: Untreated water from wells or from surface sources.

Regenerant: The solution used to restore the activity of an ion exchanger. Acids are employed to restore a cation exchanger to its hydrogen form; brine solutions may be used to convert the cation exchanger to the sodium form. The anion exchanger may be rejuvenated by treatment with an alkaline solution.

Regeneration: Restoration of the activity of an ion exchanger by replacing the ions adsorbed from the treated solution by ions that were adsorbed initially on the resin.

Reverse deionization: The use of an anion exchange unit and a cation exchange unit—in that order—to remove all ions from solution.

Rinse: The operation which follows regeneration; a flushing out of excess regenerant solution.

Siliceous gel zeolite: A synthetic, inorganic exchanger produced by the aqueous reaction of alkali with aluminum salts.

Static system: The batch-wise employment of ion exchange resins, wherein (since ion exchange is an equilibrium reaction) a definite end-point is reached involving fixed ratios of ion distribution between the resin and solution.

Sulfonic: A specific acidic group (SO_3H) on which depends the exchange activity of certain cation adsorbents.

Swelling: The expansion of an ion exchange bed which occurs when the reactive groups on the resin are converted into certain forms.

Throughput volume: The amount of solution passed through an exchange bed before exhaustion of the resin is reached.

Upflow: The operation of an ion exchange unit in which solutions are passed in at the bottom and out at the top of the container.

Voids: The space between the resinous particles in an ion exchange bed.

Zeolite: Naturally-occurring hydrous silicates exhibiting limited base exchange.

Index

163